DOUGLAS JESUS ME

A Letter to a Christian Atheist

Russel Moffat

British Library Cataloguing in Publication Data:
a catalogue record for this publication
is available from the British Library

ISBN   978-1-912052-64-6

The right of Russel Moffat to be identified as the author of
this work has been asserted by him in accordance with the
Copyright, Designs and Patents Act 1988

Typeset in 11.5pt Minion Pro at Haddington, Scotland

Printed by Short Run Press Ltd, Exeter

Contents

Introduction   1

Chapter 1   Conflicted and Confused   5

Chapter 2   Biblical Criticism   13

Chapter 3   Something Happened Here   24

Chapter 4   The Voice of God   43

Chapter 5   Future Orientation: "Still Dreaming
                                     Christian Dreams"   52

Chapter 6   The Christ and his Kingdom: Changing
                                          Worldviews   61

To all of God's prodigals and pilgrims:
may you find bread for the journey
and grace for the moment

Introduction

Dear Douglas,

We have never met but I am an admirer of your work. For many years I have read your articles and books and watched and heard many an interview on YouTube, TV and Radio. You are one of the reasons that I am a subscriber to the Spectator. So thanks for that.

There is no presumption or expectation on my part of a reply to this or any ongoing correspondence between us, and any familiarity in tone is only a response to your affable persona mediated through your public discourse. I am writing this simply because I cannot do otherwise; a feeling I'm sure you have experienced yourself on many occasions.

I am a minister in the Church of Scotland and therefore have always been fascinated by the intersection of your life and thought with religious matters. Let me make it clear at the outset that this is not a polemical or evangelical work. I do not intend to 'sort you out' or challenge the prodigal to 'come home'. I have enough problems with myself. I write as one 'lonely man of faith' (appropriating the title of Rabbi Joseph Soloveitchik's famous book) to someone I perceive to be another 'lonely man of faith' and with whom I want share some thoughts. I have heard you described as a wounded exile who needs to return to fold. That may well be true but we are all 'exiles' in one way or another and there is no permanent refuge this side of the great divide. Our Jewish friends are rich both in stories and in sayings. One of the latter is that the people of Israel are 'chosen to live between the fires of this world' and another is a prayer, 'Lord could we be a little less chosen!'

These two sentiments don't need commentary but they do tap into the hopeful melancholy and paradoxical heart of religious belief, particularly in the Judeo-Christian tradition.

In so many ways, it is obvious that you have found your calling/vocation in life and we are the beneficiaries of that. No doubt there is a cost to being a public intellectual, particularly a controversial one, but you handle it well. You are a much needed cultural and political critic in our day and age and your voice is often a wonderful antidote to some of the nonsense in our contemporary society. I believe the power of that voice comes not just from a sharp intellect examining complex issues but also from a sensitive heart which you sometimes wear on your sleeve. This makes you an appealing character in contrast to many of our 'armour wearing' contemporary politicians and activists of all shades.

I wrote this response during this past year of global pandemic and as we begin to feel our way forward out of lockdown. These last months have been, to quote John Lennon, 'strange days indeed'. I have appreciated your comments and critique of the Churches' handling of the crisis although that was mainly in relation to the Church of England.

Opinions vary without and within the churches regarding the future of Faith, post Covid. For some, this will prove to be the last nail in the coffin for an already dying and decaying institution that is well past its 'sell by' date. For others, these last months may prove to be the springboard we need for renewal and revitalisation with the recent success of online representation and the interest shown from those who are not members or regular attenders. Of course, there is some truth in both of these views although I tend to err on the side of the first. For the Christian Church, this pandemic and subsequent lockdown comes on the back of many decades of societal irrelevance, dramatic decline and demographic meltdown. Faced with the current situation, many in the Church appear bewildered and bemused, even depressed and disillusioned, not sure what to think or how to respond. I'm reminded of a phrase by the Roman historian Polybius who, when commenting on the battle of Lake Trasimene where the Carthaginians led by the famous General Hannibal overwhelmed the Roman army, said of the Legions, 'Death overtook them while they wondered what to do.' Sounds like the contemporary Church to me!

But death and resurrection are at the heart of the Christian faith. Whilst standing amidst the ruins of Christendom, it is rewarding to review the incredible history of the Christian church, warts and all, and remind ourselves that things wax and wane. The 'forgotten' or even better, 'unknown' Church of the East, thrived for a millennium stretching from Syria to China at its zenith. For centuries it has been in radical decline thanks among other things to Mongol and Islamist persecution. The death blow to the remaining remnant was administered by Isis in recent years.

This should remind us that there is nothing invulnerable or sacrosanct about Western Christianity *per se* and it could go the same way albeit in a different context and for different reasons. That thought has to be balanced up with the global expansion of the Christian Faith in Africa, parts of Asia, and South America. The centre of gravity in ecclesiastical terms has been changing for some time. So to appropriate a phrase from REM, 'It's the end of the world as we know it and I feel fine.' That said, I'm not ready to give up completely on the Western Church just yet.

Over these last years I have been fascinated by your openness about faith and religion. Your honesty and realism is both refreshing and challenging. As I understand it you were a member of the Anglican Church in your younger days and even a 'believer' at times. Subsequently, that changed and you have been described and, indeed, self-identified, with a number of terms from 'Cultural Christian,' and 'Aesthetic Anglican,' to 'Christian Atheist.' But, it must be said, you seem to find it hard to completely let go. Rightly or wrongly, I sense a touch of melancholy and wistfulness in some of the things you say and especially the way you say them. I stand to be corrected if I have got that wrong. I note that you have not gone down the road of your friends the late Christopher Hitchens and the ever present Sam Harris and have recently described yourself as a 'supporter from the outside' when it comes to the Christian Church. The public positioning of yourself somewhere between Sam and Jordan Peterson in their recent popular debates, which you moderated, is itself quite revealing and from my perspective, very welcome. Of course, if your friend Richard Dawkins is right then you are still recovering from the after-effects of the 'virus' of religion, which, it seems, is a lot more virulent in the cultural realm than Covid-19 is in the biological realm. This, it could be argued, is demonstrated by your apparent lack of clarity and clear conviction on these matters. But for me, this is a hopeful sign and it is here that I want to respond to some of the things you have said and written. I will work in concentric circles from the particular to the general, from the personal to the practical and share with you something of my own journey.

Chapter 1

Conflicted and Confused!

You wrote recently that on matters of religion you were 'conflicted' and 'confused.'[1]

I admire your honesty and I am actually pleased to hear that. Join the club!

Although, I have to say, that is quite a different tone from 2009 and the quiet confidence of your (then) new-found and apparently liberating atheism is it not?[2] My first response is a question. Is there anything wrong with being 'conflicted' and 'confused?' History and personal experience surely demonstrate that 'certainty' in the ideologies of religion and politics can be lethal, if not evil, particularly if allied to power. I wish more people had doubts about what they 'believe' or don't 'believe'; it would surely make the world a more interesting and friendly place.

Besides, does your own confession, noted above, not put you in very good company? It places you in the ranks of many a philosopher (particularly existentialist) and many a Christian thinker, theologian, and even saint. The ever quotable G.K. Chesterton once said only 'materialists and madmen never have doubts'. I am also reminded of Dostoevsky's statement, 'It is not as a child that I believe and confess Jesus Christ. My hosanna is born of a furnace of doubt.' Or, if you want a less dramatic, contemporary, and secular example, Michael Palin, who shares your love of visiting churches, describes himself as 'an agnostic with doubts.'[3] All of course, wonderful stuff! In the Gospels, the disciples seemed to have been pretty 'conflicted' and 'confused' most of the time

---

1 *Spectator Magazine*, 18th July 2020.

2 *Spectator Magazine*, 3rd January 2009.

3 Michael Palin, *50 Things to do in a Church* – YouTube.

but they stayed the course on that roller-coaster ride of following Jesus. I personally find some comfort in that. I would surmise that wrestling with faith and doubt has been standard fare throughout history even, or especially, when it could not be voiced publicly.

I am a 'man of faith' (to use a line from a Neil Diamond song) and that faith has continually inspired, challenged and frustrated me over the years. It has been an ever-changing, yet ever-green, constituent of my innermost being. I cannot be understood apart from it and I certainly cannot imagine life without it. Over the years my divided self has known what it is like to walk the tightrope between faith and doubt, obedience and rebellion, service and survival – although as the great Karl Wallenda said, 'Being on a tightrope is living; everything else is waiting.' Changing metaphors, it has been a challenging path that I have walked with many mountain top 'highs' and many dark valley 'lows'.

Along the way, I have experienced 'extreme fluctuations' (Charles Darwin) and even 'desperate disquiets' (John Bunyan). Sometimes my tide has been in 'melancholy retreat' (Thomas Arnold) but at other times it has been in full flow: vital, vibrant, and visceral, especially when inspired by the prose of St Paul. These tensions have been heightened and the anguish exacerbated, by the inhabiting of two separate but related domains: the vocational and the academic. As a clergyman I have had a leadership and pastoral role within a specific religious institution with the constrained duties of teaching, exhorting, encouraging and comforting the faithful. On the other hand, in my own academic research and, subsequently, as a part-time University tutor, I had the freedom to ask the difficult and awkward questions, the opportunity to think 'outside the box', and the perfect environment in which to challenge and test my faith. These two worlds and, indeed, two roles, are not always happy bed-fellows; hence the existential struggle that has characterised my life and which has often led to conflicting emotions and moods. The late controversial historian A.J.P. Taylor used to say that he 'held extreme views very weakly.' I can identify with that. Like Plato, I believe in the pursuit of the

Good, the True and the Beautiful, but like Pilate before Christ, I find myself continually asking – with no small amount of perplexity and even cynicism – 'What is truth?' When I was younger, things were a lot more black and white, but as the years have passed, it is not just my hair that has turned grey. Yet my muddled mind often disappoints and frustrates my passionate heart. It seems that I need something to believe in and commit my life to – it is just the way I'm constituted – but sustaining such with any semblance of power and perseverance over time can be an uphill battle.

It was Nietzsche who said, 'There are no facts only interpretations.' The best counter to this statement is a line from the TV series *Taggart* where the tough-talking Glasgow Detective responds to an obnoxious academic type with the quip, 'That is why Nietzsche never made Detective!' A pragmatic no-nonsense answer indeed! Yet, as the years roll by, the more I feel the force in the great philosopher's aphorism (I confess that goes for a lot of Nietzscheanisms). I have come to appreciate the wise advice that 'what reason can construct, reason can refute'. So true, but often quite disconcerting and challenging to the point, sometimes, of exhaustion. At the beginning of his best-selling book *A Road less Travelled*, M. Scott Peck states that 'life is difficult'. At the beginning of his follow up work, *Further Along The Road Less Travelled*, he adds that 'life is complex'.

I unhesitatingly concur with both of these designations but would add a third which is a consequence of the first two. Life is therefore 'messy!' Because of this I am extremely wary of all forms of fundamentalism (and they are not all religious by any means!) None of us have truth 'boxed' and reality 'tamed'. During the Second World War, the German General Erwin Rommel, was charged with defending the so-called Atlantic Wall against Allied invasion. On inspection trips to the defences he would often ask officers to remove their gloves. If there were no signs of scarring or wear and tear visible on their hands from building up the fortifications they were demoted on the spot for failing to lead by example. My scars are not on my hands but on my soul. To those I meet who claim to be engaged with the 'ultimate' issues of life and who display no doubt, angst or existential travail, I have very little to say. Life is too short for that! But I detect in you, in part at least, a kindred spirit; hence this response.

My problem is quite simply where else would I go? Having inhabited the Christian worldview for so many years I see nothing else that remotely attracts me as a viable option. During the First World War there was a famous cartoon character called 'Old Alf'. In one scene, Alf, a veteran of the fighting, is depicted sheltering in a shell-hole with a rather green conscript whilst under German artillery fire. The young soldier complains about their situation and old Alf replies, 'Well if you can find a better shell-hole go crawl to it.' I am very aware of the provisional character of my worldview and hence the vulnerability of my faith construction. However, it is the best that I can do within the contingencies, challenges and constraints of personal experience and knowledge.

This brings me to that word which causes a negative reaction in some places – 'faith'. It is such a maligned, misunderstood and misused term with conflation and confusion often being present in the contexts where it is used or criticised. For the redoubtable and eternally quotable Mark Twain, faith was defined as 'believing what you know ain't so'. In the film *Philadelphia* there is a scene early on where Andy (Tom Hanks), on being promoted, thanks his Boss for having 'faith in him'. His Boss replies in Dawkinesque style, 'Faith, Andy, is a belief in something for which we have no evidence. It does not apply in this situation.' However, later on in the film, after Andy is diagnosed with Aids and his sexual orientation is revealed, his Boss accuses him of 'breaking the trust placed in him'. Confused? The script writer certainly was.

In the New Testament story, faith is portrayed as personal, relational, and existential. When the first disciples followed Jesus they were exercising basic 'trust' – a common and universal phenomenon in human affairs and interactions. They freely committed themselves to an 'adventure' in partnership with him. The characteristics of courage, honesty and openness were essential for the integrity of that enterprise. For them Jesus was not just some random guy who happened to be passing by one day out of the blue. This didn't take place in a vacuum but in a very particular context. Presumably they already knew certain things about the man from Nazareth and there must have been something intriguing, challenging and attractive about both his personality, and his teaching, for this initial commitment to take place. In the course of time, that trust was deepened and strengthened, and through their shared experiences, they came to believe certain things about him and were compelled to interpret what was taking place in a specific and unique way.

Faith for me can be defined as 'the orientation of the self towards life and reality in the light of knowledge and experience.' It is a way of perceiving the world and responding to it. But that orientation has to start somewhere in time and space. At the hub of the Christian 'wheel' is the person of Jesus, and the Christian worldview is constructed from the story of ancient Israel and of Jesus of Nazareth, both found in the biblical narrative. This reminds us that religious faith is always 'earthed' somewhere, it is never 'free-floating' – whatever such a concept would mean in practice.

Now I know that you apparently see yourself as a supporter of the Church from the 'outside'. I hope you don't mind if I see you differently. All religions are very large circles of faith and there is usually a considerable distance between the centre and the circumference. I would put you near the outer perimeter but still within the circle. Actually Douglas, you kind of put yourself there by what you say and do. In this regard I would not consider you to be in the same category as for example, Stephen Fry, who also, I am led to believe, appreciates the beauty of church buildings and church music but who I don't think is a 'friend' of Christianity in the manner you appear to be. By the way, that is not a critical judgment of Mr Fry, whom I also respect, admire and like. It is only an observation: one which, once again, I stand to be corrected on.

I have been the minister of five different congregations over the years and they have all contained a variety of people from card carrying, credal espousing members all the way to agnostics and even the odd 'occasional' atheist. The latter were people who were sometimes atheist depending on which week you met them just as there were others who were sometimes Christian depending on when you encountered them! Human beings are such fabulous non-conformists it makes life wonderfully interesting. I think the Divine must have a great sense of humour.

I acknowledge that one of the areas of concern and struggle for you is how we relate to the Bible in this modern age and I intend to deal with biblical criticism in the next chapter. So, what follows will prepare the ground for that with some preliminary comments. Many homes in the UK will have a Bible somewhere in the house but it will be hidden away in a drawer or being used to press flowers or even hold a door open.

I was intrigued to see that it became Norway's bestselling book recently when the first Norwegian translation in thirty years went on sale in October 2011. By the end of the year, 80,000 copies had already been sold with queues forming at the shops. Quite an amazing phenomenon in this day and age, but doubly so in the context of the often quoted Scandinavian secularity. I'm sure that many of our atheist friends would have been surprised with this news-item and the headlines it generated. Yet I am very curious to know the reasons for this, and how many of these purchasers actually got round to reading the book they had so purposefully obtained. I would also be intrigued to know from those who did attempt to read it just exactly what they thought of the content. The evidence would seem to suggest that Bible readers can end up very perplexed and bewildered by the experience. Which is maybe one of the reasons that many folks are just content to own a copy but keep it safely quarantined. That the Bible is a foundational document for the Christian Faith goes without saying, but it seems that many of the 'faithful' seem to know either next to nothing about it, or, alternatively, are very partial in what they do know.

We live in a sound-bite age and many Christians only know the Bible through a handful of favourite verses, selected texts, or popular stories. For some, to read the Bible as literature is to 'fall down the rabbit hole' (Alice in Wonderland) and enter a strange new world quite alien to our own and a million miles away from our modern perceptions and experiences. It is a world of the supernatural, the miraculous, and the weirdly ritualistic. For others, it is to encounter a violent story or, series of stories, which can offend our sensibilities and ideas of justice and fairness. Not only God, but many of the heroic biblical characters, are depicted in ways that we struggle to equate with best of our contemporary values and norms. In fact, one atheist blogger recently suggested that the best way to undermine faith was to encourage Christians to actually read their Holy Book! Of course true, but only one side of the coin. There is also a positive case to be made.

The title of U2's famous album 'All That You Can't Leave Behind' provides us with the appropriate sentiments here. Despite its failings and limitations, the Bible is something the Church cannot abandon as it confronts and adapts to this 'brave new world' of ours. Rather it is a 'treasure' we have to learn to appreciate and utilise critically, realistically, and honestly. However, before we can do that, we must first review the historical backdrop to these issues which I will do briefly in the following chapter. For now, I want to use an illustration to set the scene for that and to delineate where I am coming from myself.

My proposal for our relationship to Scripture is best described with the following metaphor used many years ago by John Stott the late Evangelical Anglican. It goes something like this. A Fundamentalist is like a caged bird which has the potential to fly but not the freedom to use it. There is no liberty to question and explore. On the other hand, a Liberal is like a gas-filled balloon which rises into the air entirely unrestrained from the earth. It has the freedom to soar but has no anchorage or directional capabilities and eventually disappears from view. However, the Evangelical is like a kite which can fly great distances, soar to great heights, perform superb acrobatics and 'dance on the wind' whilst all the time having an anchor point at ground level. In all three cases it is the relationship or lack of with the Scriptures, which is the crucial point.

I love this illustration but acknowledge that the terms Liberal and Evangelical can be problematic as they both cover broad categories of people. For me the third grouping consists of those who have not cut themselves off completely from the Christian Scriptures but who, in the light of the best of Church tradition and modern thought, creatively interact with this wonderful biblical legacy that was generated within believing and faithful communities and bequeathed to us. It is a 'living' text, perennially powerful, relevant and indispensable for the Church of today as it makes its way in the world.

That brings me to important questions regarding literature and history as they relate to the Christian story. I will do this in the light of other comments you have made.

Chapter 2

Biblical Criticism – Friend or Foe?

In the 2009 article already cited above you wrote – 'Charles Darwin didn't do for God. German biblical criticism did.' I know what you were trying to say but I need to tweak this a bit. You are right on the first part. Darwin didn't do for God. If the writer of Genesis 1 has primary and secondary causation built into the fabric of his text (cf. generative powers of the waters and the earth vv. 20, 24) and if the theological discussion of the relationship of God's providence in relation to contingent events goes back as far as Augustine, then it is no surprise why Victorian society could so quickly embrace Darwin. The theological tools were there to do so. Besides, the ground for a broadening of horizons both scientifically and biblically had already been prepared by the proponents of the new geology in the late 18th and early 19th centuries, most, if not all of whom, were devout Christians. Furthermore, in 19th century upper class minds, the term 'evolution' had radical political and social implications post-French Revolution. That concern, not religious ones *per se,* was often in the background of the debates of the time.

Moving on, I'm not sure about the second sentence of your quote. The Deists of the 18th and 19th centuries had many problems with the Bible and with religion in general but they still believed in a Creator. So the development of biblical criticism didn't 'do for God' but certainly seemed to challenge religion based on revelation, in particular Christianity. But even here, qualifications are needed. German biblical criticism was a product of the Reformation and the Enlightenment. The latter term is hard to define as a period and a movement, and seems to centre on a cluster of attitudes and ideas in 18th century Europe.[4]

It is a term often used and magnified by atheists and secularists as the antithesis of all things religious. However, the Enlightenment was a protest emerging from a protest and the ground for it was definitely laid by the Reformation. The slogan 'Dare to think for yourself' (Kant), often used to epitomise the Enlightenment, represented the Protestant ethos exactly.

Furthermore, the dynamic principle of *Ecclesia Reformata, Semper Reformanda* (the church reformed, always reforming), encouraged the spirit of critical enquiry and Protestants were especially open to influence from new ideas and, indeed, in turn, helped to shape them. A lack of a centralised ecclesiastical structure allowed greater freedom for creative thought and the new emphasis on teaching and the need for well-educated clergy resulted in a close relationship between Protestantism and the Universities.

In addition, it has been argued that the rise of modern science was linked to the Protestant approach to texts. In this view the switch from the ahistorical, symbolical and allegorical understanding of the Scriptures dominant in the Middle Ages to an historical and literal one, laid the foundations for a completely new way of looking at reality. This calls into question the common myth that as people began to look at the world differently (science) they were compelled to view the Bible differently. It now seems it was the other way around. Because the Bible was read differently, the world was seen differently.[5]

Of course, all of this was a two-edged sword. Being creative and critical is great when exploring, defending or sustaining the faith; not so good when the tables are turned and faith itself is under the spotlight. In this regard it could be said that Protestantism sowed the seeds of its own undermining.

---

4 Alister McGrath, *Christian Theology*, Blackwell 2001, pp. 89ff.

5 Peter Harrison, *The Territories of Science and Religion*, University of Chicago Press 2017.

In fostering individualism and rejecting the Papacy and the authority of the church, Protestantism needed the authority of the Scriptures to fill the foundational vacuum left by the Reformation. But when some scholars in the name of 'Reason' and 'Historical Criticism' found the Bible wanting in this regard, there were of course problems. But let's not overblow this. When all is said and done we are still here. For the last two hundred years, the Christian church has been adapting, in varying degrees, to the rise of modern biblical criticism. It has, in a variety of ways, adopted and absorbed many of the challenges thrown up by this. But then, why wouldn't that be the case, since Christians have done that from the beginning? Contrary to the caricature, faith is not a static, blind, entrenched, and infantile entity: it is, rather, a process – a dynamic, open, developing and maturing one. Or at least it should be – it is *meant* to be! In the words of the Apostle Paul:

> When I was a child, I spoke like a child; I thought like a child, I reasoned like a child. But when I became a man, I put childish things behind me. (1 Corinthians 13:11)

To be mature in our understanding was a key theme in Paul's letters. His own life exemplified that principle. Through encounter and experience, followed by reflection and engagement, Paul wrestled long, hard and sometimes painfully, with events and issues which were, ultimately, life-transforming. Challenge and change were essential ingredients in his intellectual journey and theological development.

The contemporary 'cultured despisers' of religion (sometimes referred to as the New Atheists) make many criticisms of religion but three in particular stand out. It is claimed that faith is intrinsically incorrigible, irrational, and immoral.[6] The first of these relates to the accusation that religion is impervious to criticism being based on revelation, authority and tradition.

---

6 See the assorted works of Richard Dawkins, Daniel Dennett, Sam Harris and Christopher Hitchens.

This leads to a lack of openness, honesty and realism. It stultifies critical thought and makes religious institutions impervious to change. Now, all of that is partly true, both historically and contemporaneously, but it is by no means the whole truth. In reviewing the recent literature on this it becomes apparent that religious people like me can't win. If we maintain our faith in the face of modernity we are accused of intellectual stupidity in holding to a belief system that is hopelessly dated, irrelevant and unable to change with the flow of history. If, on the other hand, we try to modify and reform our faith in the light of new intellectual challenges, we are accused of hypocrisy and intellectual dishonesty![7]

Throughout its history, the Christian faith has often been in competition and/or conflict with various other religions, ideologies and philosophies. From the scathing attacks of Celsus and Lucian to Voltaire and Gibbons, from Nietzsche, Marx, and Freud to Richard Dawkins, the Christian faith has had to reflect long and hard on its core beliefs and *raison d'être*. From the beginning, theology has attempted to both articulate and justify Christian belief and practice, and from Justin to Origin, Augustine to Calvin, and Schleiermacher to Barth, it has done that with varying degrees of success and failure. This is still a work in progress and the story goes on. Throughout its history the Church has had to cope not just with intellectual revolutions but with the sometimes massive political, economic and cultural changes that have often accompanied them. Once again the Church has learned with varying degrees of success and failure to adapt to these situations. Therefore, the contemporary twin challenges of biblical criticism and Darwinian evolution have to be viewed in this context.

When I went to University in 1980, biblical studies were still to some extent dominated by German scholars. But even then things were changing. We used to joke that 'theology was created

---

7 Sam Harris in particular seems to believe that religious moderates are either disingenuous or dishonest, as he has made clear in many interviews and talks and Q/A's.

in Germany, corrected in Britain and corrupted in the United States.' Germany most certainly doesn't dominate the theological scene now, and times have changed. I am happy to report that I survived my University education (including a Masters and Doctorate in the 90s) and have been a minister for 34 years. German historical criticism didn't do me any harm. Okay! I do admit that as a conservative Christian at that time, I did wince and recoil a bit in first year, but I soon got over it. This was partly because those who taught me were devout men and women and, as I subsequently discovered, so were many of these Germans! The anti-Christian, anti-religion side of historical biblical criticism particularly in the 19th century did not carry all before it. We are all 'children of our time' and inhabit very particular socio-intellectual worlds. The agendas and methods of biblical criticism in the 16th to the 21st centuries display marked variations and emphases as scholars were, and still are, responding to their own situation in life. How could it have been otherwise? But through it all, that vast sprawling book called the Bible continues to be relevant and inspirational.

I remember hearing an atheist contributor in a debate on the BBC's *Big Questions* show hosted by Nicky Campbell, state that the Bible nowhere displayed philosophy as good as Plato, science as good as Newton and literature as good as Shakespeare. A brilliant soundbite. All of which is true (although some may quibble about the third of these propositions) but, I may add, totally irrelevant. All three of these together have not impacted history the way the Bible has. How many people worldwide today, gather together regularly in the respective names of that triad? The Bible is commonly dismissed contemptuously as a Bronze Age document. This is a bit unfair as it is primarily an Iron Age book! It is also, despite the condescension of our contemporary 'cultured despisers' of religion, still a 'living text' second to none.

One of the flaws in 19th century historical criticism was the naïve assumption of the possibility of 'autonomous reason' and of the scholar of texts as being an unencumbered objective interpreter; a simple 'non-partisan' and 'uninvolved reader' of data. But scholarship is never neutral: it can't be. It is theory-laden and in practice ideological. How could it not be? The best we can hope for is to be conscious of our assumptions and presuppositions. Lastly, trends, models, and modes, of biblical interpretation continue to change and currents come and go. The 'fetish of methodology' rages in our contemporary world and that includes biblical studies. When I hear the seemingly endless list of hyphenated 'xx- criticisms' used these days in biblical studies, I lose the will to live and thank God for the 1980s. Anyway Douglas, back to you.

In the 2009 article mentioned at the start of this section you wrote, 'Realising that "holy" texts are, like most other things in life, the result of an accretion of human effort and human error is one of the most troubling discoveries any believer can make.' Really? On the contrary I find it liberating. In that article you were informing readers that is was studying Islam that made you an atheist. I'll ignore the apparent *non sequitur* in that position and instead concentrate on textual matters. The Bible is not the Qur'an and both Jews and Christians do not generally and historically speaking approach textual matters as Muslims do. For starters, when was the last time you handled a Bible? Did you wash your hands first, as Muslims do before picking up a Qur'an? Why not? Well because Christians don't do that. It is not the 'book' that is holy. The Qur'an refers to Jews and Christians as 'People of the Book' (e.g. Surah 5). That is inaccurate and, indeed, misleading.

The Hebrew Bible has 36 'books' (Christian Bibles arrange them into 39) divided into three concentric circles with different levels of importance. First, the *Torah* (Law) then the *Nevi'im* (Prophets) and lastly, the *Ketuvim* (Writings). The New Testament has 27 different 'books' but the first level of importance goes to the four Gospels. Therefore, a nuanced approach is needed when comparing the Semitic faiths. For Muslims the Qur'an is literally the 'word of God'; not written by Muhammed but channelled through him. Every word in the Qur'an is holy. A truly faithful and devout Muslim is expected to learn Arabic as a result (and it must be said that a devout Jew is supposed to learn Hebrew). That is definitely not the case in Christianity. I have not once in my years as a minister instructed a parishioner to learn Greek in order to read the Gospels although such an enterprise is undoubtedly rewarding. At another level, it should be noted that for Christians the 'Word of God' is a Person (Jesus) not a book. The Scriptures *point* to the 'Word of God' they are not in themselves the 'Word of God.' These are distinctions which have major implications.

Enlightenment thinkers developed the proposal that the Bible had a complexity of layers to it with many books revealing multiple sources which have been composed and redacted over time. They also pointed out internal contradictions in many of the texts. They therefore insisted that the Bible should be analysed and evaluated like any other piece of literature. But consider this quote from Benjamin Jowett the Victorian Master of Balliol College Oxford in 1860:

> *When interpreted like any other book, by the same rules of evidence and the same canons of criticism, the Bible will still remain unlike any other book; its beauty will be freshly seen, as a picture which is restored after many ages to its original state; it will create a new interest and make for itself a new kind of authority by the life which is in it. It will be a spirit and not a letter; as it was in the beginning, having an influence like that of the spoken word, or the book . . . newly found.*[8]

The main problem with German higher criticism was the internal propulsion of the discipline to 'atomise' scriptural texts through an over-rigorous use of a variety of analytical methodologies. This happened incrementally and cumulatively over time. The resultant 'dissection' was, ultimately, too severe and the 'living patient' died on the operating table. Unfortunately, this undermined the fruits and gains resulting from a forensic and scientific approach to the interpretation of an ancient document of which there were many.

---

8 A.H. Hart, *Strangers and Pilgrims Once More*, Eerdmans 2014, p. 57.

As a 'Romantic' response to the 'Rationalism' of Enlightenment thought, the quote above from Jowett strikes a chord. In the 18ᵗʰ century, emotionalism was a parallel and counterpoise to the hegemony of reason. The Romantic emphasis on the artistic and aesthetic sense of the text fed into Liberal Protestant thought with J.G. Hamann claiming that 'poetry' was the 'mother speech' of humanity.[9]

Incidentally, I think that this historic divide between the head and the heart, reason and imagination, is a phenomenon which will continue to run on into the future and a bridge between these two differing but essential fundamentals, needs to be built especially from a Christian point of view. But is this approach (Bible as literature) enough? I don't think so. The Bible is not a book of historiography, that is obvious; but neither is it to be separated completely from history. The Bible is essentially a book of testimony concerning the 'miracle' and 'mystery' of Israel and the 'miracle' and 'mystery' of Jesus of Nazareth. The provocative terminology is deliberate. A lifetime of engagement is necessary to unpack this amazing epic and that will include *both* historical analysis and creative imagination in understanding the Bible as 'story'.

Of course when we think of biblical interpretation, the question of religious Fundamentalism raises its unwelcome head. Unquestionably the conservative wing of Protestantism became more entrenched as it responded to the critical thought emerging from the Enlightenment, a phenomenon which was exacerbated by the later controversies around Darwin. Unfortunately, we are still living with this today. The ideal of pristine purity and original unity is a myth for all major religions. As in the realm of politics there has existed from time immemorial 'hawks' and 'doves', so too in religion, there have always been conservatives and moderates. This divide is even found within the Bible itself.

---

9 G.W. Bromiley, *Historical Theology: An Introduction*, T and T Clark 1978, p. 349.

It is a myth that once upon a time, especially in the beginning, all Christians believed exactly the same things and the understanding of sacred texts was a straightforward process of literal interpretation based on the proposition 'When the plain sense makes sense we seek no other sense' (a quotation beloved by American Fundamentalists). This is always accompanied by the second myth that it was only in the age of Godless modernity that embarrassed and cowardly liberal believers made compromises with the faith and indulged in exegetical contortions to re-interpret the Bible. Something also endorsed by atheists like Sam Harris (very convenient for him).

The final myth from a Christian point of view is the promulgation of the notion that if we could only 'return' to the thought world of that Golden Age everything would be alright. Paradoxically, it can be argued that Christian Fundamentalism in its contemporary manifestation represents the illegitimate child of the Enlightenment not the return of the prodigal son to the family home. Fundamentalism is a particular kind of religion before it is a system of literary interpretation and exegesis. It is based on a model abstracted from the Scriptures through selective interpretation; one which meets the psychological needs of a particular mind set. This model is then bolstered and protected by a specific doctrine of the Scriptures which appears to give that model authority and legitimacy but which is itself a part of the model. Subsequent interpretation involves processing the Bible through the funnel of that creed which then flattens out all the rich and rewarding diversity of the biblical texts.

The Bible is not a perfect and pristine book. What would that even look like and how would we know it was? It did not float down from the skies in a parachute bound in black leather with a zip at the side and the words 'King James Bible' written on the cover. Instead the Bible represents an evolving and developing tradition over a long period. It is like a snowball rolling through time which accumulates increasing amounts of snow alongside bits and pieces of debris along the way (a metaphor I owe to my former Hebrew

Bible tutor Professor William Johnstone). The Bible's various parts emerged out of the religio-political complexities of the Ancient Near East and its story was characterised by debate, struggle and disagreement as well as development. All of this was accumulated along the way as the literary record grew larger.

The Scriptures of the Old and New Testaments are narratives of 'experimental' religion: of feeling the way; of grasping after truth, purpose and meaning. In the canonical texts that we have there are multiple 'voices'. There is testimony: there is counter-testimony. There are competing perspectives from priests, prophets, mystics, poets, evangelists and apostles. There are moderates and militants, conformists and rebels, traditionalists and radicals, orthodox, and dare I say it, heretics too! (How did the book of Ecclesiastes ever get canonised?)

Our Bible gives us different answers to many important questions and different perspectives on fundamental issues. It is a continual process of interpretation, reinterpretation and reapplication of the religious tradition by the religious community at various times, for various reasons, in a variety of contexts. It is a 'log' book not an 'answer' book. It is not an ancient version of Google! It is a resource book for faith but not for all types of problem solving. It does not furnish the believer with a complete set of propositional truths giving authoritative guidance on *all matters* of life. Rather it reveals something of the experience and knowledge of others who have gone before us in the faith and therefore acts as a springboard of inspiration for our own personal and collective adventure of faith in the present.

It is critical here to realise that vigorous debates within the Jewish and Christian communities over the centuries concerning the meaning of faith is also mirrored within the Scriptures themselves. The engagement is not all one way i.e. God with humans. On the contrary, as noted above, it invariably involves humans engaging/wrestling with other humans, sometimes vigorously, *about* God and the meaning of it all. For example, differences and tensions clearly existed between the Priests and

Prophets in Ancient Israel and between Paul and James in the New Testament. Many more examples could be highlighted. All of this makes the Bible a fascinating read. It also makes it far more real and meaningful than any alleged 'infallible' and 'inerrant' document (whatever these terms actually mean in practice) ever could. This is not to run away from reality, it is to *embrace* it.

The wonderful messiness of biological evolution, human history, the Bible and my own personal life are all brought together in a unity which represents the world in which I 'live and move and have my being.' *Contra* Sam Harris, this has not been forced upon people like me by the alleged hammer blows of modernity to Christian faith. Even if Harris' caricature was right in all its details it still wouldn't matter.

Socrates famously said that 'the unexamined life is not worth living'. Likewise for Christians, I would argue that 'the unexamined faith' is not worth having. The Apostle Paul enjoins us to 'test all things and hold fast to that which is good' (1 Thessalonians 5:21). To find out that what we *have* believed is not what we *should have* believed is not to lose faith it is, following the biblical injunction to seek wisdom and understanding, to renew faith. To find out that *how* we have read the Bible is not how we *should have* read the Bible is not to discard the Bible, but to discover its power afresh.

Chapter 3

Something Happened Here!

In a recent interview and discussion with Esther O'Reilly, you mentioned that you had been on a visit to Israel in 2019 and spent a bit of time in Galilee.[10] On return to the UK a friend had asked whether you had 'felt' anything whilst there. You replied that there was a thought which you couldn't get out of your head, namely – 'something happened here!' Not an uncommon experience in the Holy Land I might add, but very interesting in your case. Can we answer that question, at least in part, in relation to the Christian faith? Well, we can try!

The phrase Jesus of Nazareth consists of two simple nouns: one a person and the other a village. Yet in combination they point to one of the greatest stories ever told in human history and present us with a conundrum from the outset. In the ancient world it was a small minority of elites who were literate. It was only the elite who were usually mentioned in literature and only towns and cities of importance that were listed too. In general terms, not only is history written by the victors, but it is also recorded by the rulers and those in authority in the upper levels of the social and political hierarchy. Therefore, the fact that 'Jesus' and 'Nazareth' are not only mentioned in an ancient document but mentioned in conjunction with each other is a pretty remarkable fact.

Nazareth was a peasant village in Galilee, the type of place normally excluded from written accounts. Even within the New Testament there is that wonderfully revealing comment by Nathaniel when Philip tells him about Jesus: 'Nazareth! Can anything good come from there?' (John 1:46) If Jesus was from a peasant back-ground, it is equally remarkable that he is mentioned

---

10 'Unbelievable', *Premier Christian Radio*, 4th January 2020.

too. But there he is; alongside Augustus, Tiberius, Pilate and Herod. Further, his name in Hebrew was simply *Yeshua* – Joshua. Yes, one of the most famous characters in literature and history was simply 'Josh' from a poor, rural backwater! Who would have thought it? Who can believe it?

Two thousand years and counting, the story rumbles on. Jesus was controversial then, he is controversial now. He has been the subject of endless fascination, intrigue and debate and there is no end in sight. Even today his name generates headlines, sells millions of books, produces Hollywood Films, and countless, and seemingly endless, TV documentaries. N.T. Wright notes:

> *The land of Israel is a small country. You can walk its length, north to south, in a few days, and from its central mountains you can see its lateral boundaries, the sea to the west and the river to the east. But it has an importance out of all proportion to its size. Empires have fought over it. Every forty-four years out of the last four thousand, on average, an army has marched through it . . . The New Testament has not been around as long as the land of Israel, but in other ways there are remarkable parallels. It is a small book, smaller than anybody else's holy book, small enough to be read through in a day or two. But it has had an importance belied by its slim appearance. It has again and again been a battle-ground for warring armies.*[11]

As for the land of his birth, and as for the book containing the affirmations of his followers, so too, for Jesus himself. He has been the focus of unrivalled interest and unparalleled investigation. Warring factions have fought over him, even for him, and many have claimed him as their own even secularists and humanists. Richard Dawkins famously wore a T-shirt with the caption 'Atheists for Jesus', highlighting the point made by many before him that Jesus, stripped of the supernatural elements of course, was someone who can be respected, even admired. For Dawkins, Jesus was one of history's great 'ethical innovators', a man who was ahead of his time.

---

11 N.T. Wright, *The New Testament and the People of God*, SPCK 1992, p. 3.

Philosopher Daniel Dennett, Dawkins friend and fellow 'Horseman' of the New Atheism, described Jesus in a radio debate as 'a good man, a clever man.' So what else can we say about him?

A secular historian's creed regarding Jesus would probably include the following:

1. Jesus was a Galilean who lived under the Roman occupation of 1st century Galilee and Judea during the reigns of the Emperors Augustus and Tiberius.

2. He was a Jewish teacher/prophet.

3. He was crucified under the Governorship of Pontius Pilate.

4. A movement which started during his life continued after his death.

This is of necessity minimalist in content and in general terms I think non-controversial. Therefore, I find the late Christopher Hitchens' view that the existence of Jesus was 'highly questionable' quite amazing, although for him, not unexpected.[12] Given the nature of the study of ancient history this degree of scepticism would present the discipline with an impossible task. Let's take an analogy from another discipline. If the extinction of the dinosaurs, iridium deposits, and evidence of a large concavity in the Yucatan peninsula point to a comet strike on earth, what does the emergence of the Christian Church and the creation of the New Testament documents point to? Were they caused by the 'impact' of a powerful personality and therefore a response to an exceptional set of circumstances generated by specific events and an influential and dynamic life? Or, alternatively, is the whole thing a fraud, a hoax and a delusion?

After a lifetime of engagement, wrestling, and personal research on this subject, I firmly believe that the first option best fits the facts. It must be stressed that this conclusion can be reached without any need to affirm the content of the Christian story. In other words, even atheists can, in principle, give

---

12 Christopher Hitchens, *God is not Great*, Atlantic Books 2007, pp. 114, 127.

assent to the existence of a historical Jesus without that being a contradiction of their atheism or scepticism regarding all things religious. For example, it is perfectly rational to believe that a charismatic preacher called Jesus of Nazareth existed in 1st century Judea/Galilee who taught very specific things without having to believe these things oneself. Or, that the followers of Jesus came to understand and interpret the significance of his life and death a particular way without feeling any compulsion to concur with their conclusions.

The first followers of Jesus drew their inspiration not from a book but from a living encounter with a person. Jesus himself never wrote a book, but seems to have so impacted the lives of other people that a community was brought into being which not only survived his death, but continued what they perceived to be his ministry and mission. It was in the promulgation of this mission – the preaching, teaching and defending of the founder and his message – that the Jesus community collected and preserved the traditions about their Master. This material was in all probability in oral form to begin with, before becoming the written sources which were subsequently utilised and edited by the Gospel writers.

Now because of the controversy created by Dan Brown's *Da Vinci Code* in the first decade of this century, something needs to be said about the Church's selection of the Canonical Gospels. The books of Matthew, Mark, Luke and John are not in the canon of the New Testament because of accident, caprice, conspiracy, political intrigue or arbitrary selection. They were chosen because the Church of the time made a sincere and genuine attempt to preserve accounts about Jesus which were thought to be authentic and credible.

It is true that in selecting these Gospels the Church also rejected others. The existence of the Gnostic Gospels seems to have caught the imagination and interest of many people in recent times. A mixture of Hollywood sensation, public love for conspiracy stories, admiration for the perceived underdogs of history, suspicion and cynicism towards institutional religion in general and the Christian church in particular, all add to the mix.

However, a simple read through of the Gospels both Canonical and Gnostic is a good place to make a judgment. They are very different in style and content. Unlike the latter, the former have a narrative form which tells the story of Jesus in dynamic and vivid ways. There is a realism here, even allowing for the miraculous and supernatural elements. They relate very much to a Jewish milieu, especially what we know of 1st century Judea/Galilee. Strikingly, the latter do not have any Passion accounts (details of the crucifixion and death of Jesus). This is quite amazing, given the probability that if Jesus was simple a mystic who had died of old age in Galilee the world would not have heard of him. It is certainly the events in Jerusalem at the climax of Jesus' ministry that give the story told by the Canonical Gospels its sharp cutting edge. Therefore, if we are looking for the personality and teachings of the so called 'historical' Jesus, we probably have a better chance of finding him in the Canonical Gospels than in their Gnostic rivals.

Put bluntly, the former have more of a 'ring of truth' about them. It must also be said at this point that the Canonical Gospels conform to the earliest credal affirmations we have regarding the Christian faith, e.g. in the letters of Paul. This was probably the main factor in the selection of these Gospels from among others.

By canonising four Gospels, the Church canonised diversity.[13] This is a very important point. There was no attempt here to provide one, uniform, and authoritative account of Jesus. This diversity has been viewed as both a gift and a problem. With regard to the latter, it was in the 2nd century that Tatian composed the Diatessaron (literally 'through the four') which attempted to weave the elements of the four Gospels into one, single, coherent and consistent narrative. The motivation for this was apologetic. The work smoothed out and harmonised apparent contradictions and discrepancies between the four canonical Gospels thus creating one seamless narrative which, no doubt, was thought to be more easily accepted as normative for all Christians. That this enterprise ultimately failed is testimony to the fact that the Church preferred,

---

13 L.T. Johnson, *The Real Jesus*, Harper Collins 1997, pp. 146ff.

whatever, the difficulties, to accept the benefits of the richer and fuller picture of Jesus provided by all four Gospel accounts. It also indicates that the Church seemed to be more concerned with the overall meaning and significance of Jesus as portrayed by the canonical authors than the absolute literal accuracy of specific details in the story. From the beginning the Christian church has been well aware of the nature of the Gospels and the tensions, problems and contradictions in the texts.

So what are the Gospels? How do we define them? Well, let us begin by stating what they are not.

First, they are not simple eye-witness accounts. These works have come down to us under the names of Matthew, Mark, Luke, and John, although we do not know for certain who the authors of these Gospels really were. The books themselves are anonymous, the names seemingly being provided by 2nd century Church tradition. Most of these accounts do not read like the testimonies of eye-witnesses, lacking the vivid reporting, colourful touches and extraneous detail which normally characterise such a genre.[14] There is often a basic terseness in the presentation of the material which may well indicate that we are dealing with traditions that have been shaped by repeated usage within the life of the first Christian communities. Scholarly analysis reveals that much of the material in the Gospels in all probability originally comprised of small independent units, sometimes only a single saying, sometimes a complete episode, and it is these that the Gospel writers have woven into a much larger coherent narrative.[15] None of this is to suggest that the Gospels do not contain material that derives, ultimately, from those who had personal first-hand experience of Jesus and the events surrounding his ministry. This certainly is the claim in Luke chapter 1. However, it is to make clear, that the Gospel writers themselves were not in that category nor are their compositions fulfilling the aims of such a genre.

---

14 Graham Stanton, *Gospel Truth?* Harper Collins 1995, pp. 52-58.

15 A.E. Harvey, *Companion to the Gospels*, Cambridge University Press 1972, p. 16.

Second, the Gospels are not biographies, at least not in the modern sense of the word; they simply lack the information and attention to detail which would be required. For example, we know next to nothing about Jesus' background and upbringing, family and working life. With minor exceptions, the whole story is more or less condensed into a few years of Jesus' adult life depending on how long we view the time-span of his ministry. It is accepted that the Gospels share some characteristics with the Greco-Roman literature of the same period but this presumably reflects conscious or even unconscious influences on the Gospel writers in regard to cultural setting rather than a major and comprehensive imitation of genre. It is clear that in regard to literary features, the Gospels are composed, indeed constructed would be a better term, around the preaching and teaching of the early Church. It is the very specific religious context of the followers of Jesus which determine focus and content in the writings of the New Testament.[16]

Third, the Gospels are not historiographies in the modern sense. It is worth reminding ourselves that the modern concept of history dates from the 19th century. This was the age of collecting 'facts' and of 'objective' investigation into what 'really happened'.[17] In this regard, although the word history (*historia* – enquiry) has been used from Greco-Roman times, ancient writers did not view their task in the same way as historians today. Their principal focus was not in reconstructing the past for its own sake, therefore they did not feel obligated to document everything in detail. This means that modern historians consulting these works can be frustrated that the information they are looking for, and would expect to be there, is often missing.

Ancient historiographies were concerned with the instruction and edification of their readers and the material was selected and shaped to that end. In other words, there was usually a moral to

16 L. Hurtardo, 'Gospel Genre', in *Dictionary of Jesus and the Gospels*, (eds. Green, McKnight, Marshal), IVP 1992, pp. 279-282.

17 Shayler Brown, *The Origins of Christianity*, Oxford University Press 1984, pp. 8, 13, 14.

be learned from their work, which of course, was the main motive in writing it. By contemporary standards, works of ancient history can be seen as propagandistic in aim, style and content. They have an agenda over and above the mere reporting of history.

There is a caveat here. Objectivity in historical investigation and analysis is an ideal to be aimed for not a practice that is easily achieved. Modern works of history can be extensively 'agenda-laden' and 'perspective-heavy' (consider the works written on the Israel/Palestine issue!). But even when this is not noticeably the case, historians can have many unconscious presuppositions that influence the selection, interpretation and presentation of data. In summary, the Gospels may share many characteristics with ancient history writings but they also differ from them in that their main agenda and overall structure is, throughout, consistently and persistently theological.

So what are the Gospels? Well without being facetious, they are precisely that – *Gospels* ('good news'). They are literary texts which seek to share what is believed to be God's 'good news' to humankind embodied in the person and work of Jesus of Nazareth. They are religious works written to teach theology and to inspire faith and they do so by narrative means. In other words they tell a 'story'. That story is shaped according to the motives, aims, and priorities of each of the Gospel writers, which of course varies. In this sense the Gospels are not dispassionate, objective works seeking to report 'what happened'; rather, they are in a real sense, propaganda. I do not use the last term pejoratively, only descriptively. There is a difference. All promotion of beliefs, values or opinions is, to some extent, propaganda, but that need not have negative connotations, especially if this is openly acknowledged and understood.

The Gospel writers start with their own theological beliefs and intentions regarding Jesus and construct their respective narratives around this. Hence, for example, the embellishments we find regarding the events in Jerusalem and the trial of Jesus. It must be emphasised though that their accounts are anything but free creations. The essential elements of the story were inherited by the Gospel writers, whose editorial freedom was therefore constrained and restricted both by the nature of the source material, and also by the experiences, convictions and needs of the faith communities to which they belonged and for whom they were writing. Nonetheless, within these parameters, they demonstrate a fairly high degree of literary art and theological creativity in their respective constructions. Therefore, the end products are far from being the 'crude carpentry' of Christopher Hitchens's jibe. Concomitant with the genre, the Gospel writers show a fair amount of flexibility (artistic licence) in the way they place and locate specific units of tradition, sayings, incidents and episodes within their own re-telling of the story. This in turn, leads to some contradictions in time, substance and place, which makes the establishment of an absolute chronology and the fixing of specific settings difficult for the historian. Reconstructions of these are always approximations.

The Gospels are not neutral works: the writers had a message to convey and they were filled with passion and conviction about the significance and importance of Jesus. They felt compelled to describe and share that conviction with others. The Gospels are, therefore, the products *of* faith and were written *from* within faith communities, *for* those faith communities. This is why Christians should never, as I have already mentioned, have a Qur'anic view of the New Testament. The latter is not the inerrant and infallible 'Word of God.' Jesus is the 'Word of God' and the testimony of scripture points not to itself, but *to Him*.

It must be stressed at this juncture, that whilst the story of Jesus contained in the Gospels accounts should not, as literary genre, be conflated and confused with historiography, it should not be completely separated or divorced from a real-life context either. To be absolutely clear, we can, with confidence, site the Jesus event within a general historical, geographical and cultural framework. We are not dealing here with Atlantis, Shangri-La or even Middle Earth. On the contrary Jerusalem, Bethlehem,

Nazareth and Jericho etc., are real geographical places and Pilate, Herod and Caiaphas *et al,* were historical personages.

In addition, the social, religious, political and cultural milieu suggested by the Gospels appears authentic from the perspective of both Greco-Roman and Jewish history with facets and features of the narrative quite plausible. An example of the distinction, yet connection, between the categories of history and story is seen in the issue of the death of Jesus. That Jesus was crucified by the Romans is as credible a fact of ancient history as one can imagine, yet the Gospels do not highlight, except incidentally, socio-political explanations for this but instead, major on its theological significance, with of course, the Cross becoming in time, the primary symbol of the new Faith which subsequently emerged.

In comparison with religious movements like Buddhism, the origins of the Christian religion are relatively accessible to historical enquiry.[18] There is a general consensus amongst New Testament scholarship that the Gospels were written somewhere between AD 65 and AD 90: in other words between 35-60 years after the death of Jesus. The Synoptic Gospels are usually dated at the near end of the scale and John somewhere at the far end. This is not a long time in comparative terms when we are speaking of sources in ancient history, especially so given that the Gospel writers seem to have, in some way, acted as editors of already existent material, some of which has a strong likelihood of going back to the time of Jesus.

Furthermore, the letters which make up an important section of the New Testament, provide an excellent resource for the existence of a Christian community in the decades following the death of Jesus and witness to very early transmitted traditions. These reveal a 'high Christology'[19] already established in the first two decades after Jesus.[20] Finally, the book of Acts, which is probably Luke's

---

18 L.T. Johnson, *op. cit.,* p. 87.

19 That is, a belief that Jesus really was divine – see Larry Hurtado, *Lord Jesus Christ,* Eerdmans 2005, which shows how soon after his lifetime the followers of Jesus were worshipping him as God.

20 For example, in Paul's first letter to the Corinthians.

second instalment, provides a useful and fascinating perspective on the expansion of the early Christian movement including its internal and external debates.

At this juncture, something should be said about oral history. Anthropological studies in oral folklore, and the preservation of sacred history in communities largely uninfluenced by literacy, have indicated that though far from being perfect and immutable, oral traditions can have a relative accuracy and reasonable longevity depending on *what* is being remembered and *why* it is being remembered. Given that the gap between Jesus and the written texts are measured in decades not centuries this is important.

Furthermore, there is, within Judaism, a widespread and prodigious tradition of Scriptural memorization which goes back to ancient times.[21] This is not to argue that the preservation of materials relating to Jesus by his followers corresponds exactly to this, but is does put the issue of oral tradition in a more positive light. Given the impact that Jesus made, it would be simply astounding if large amounts of material relating to his life and ministry had not been preserved with passion and integrity by his followers. This process would have been greatly aided and abetted by the nature of his teaching and the drama of his life. Jesus excelled in the formulation of pithy, punchy aphorisms, in vivid parables, and in the use of dramatic imagery, hyperbole, and symbolism, all of which were strikingly memorable. Also, the radical ethics of Jesus would surely have caught the imagination: his demand for a 'religion of the heart'; limitless forgiveness; love of enemies; practical non-violence; inclusion of the outcast; mercy and grace to the needy; dignity for all including women. In other words, the 'Kingdom' programme he both proclaimed and practised. This material was remembered because it was difficult to forget. Jesus also clashed with the authorities of his day both religious and political. This resulted, once again, in the creation of memorable incidents and anecdotes being preserved within the tradition.

---

21 Craig Blomberg, *The Historical Reliability of the Gospels*, IVP 1987, pp. 25-31.

Lastly, his death, not from old age or natural causes but from a brutal execution is the elephant in the room of all evaluation, interpretation and understanding of his person, mission and meaning both then and now. In life and in death, Jesus was remembered vividly and spoken of passionately. From a fairly early stage, it appears that some of the Jesus traditions were written down. Scholars have identified at least three compilations that were believed to be extant at that time. They are designated L (material peculiar to Luke); M (material peculiar to Matthew) and the most famous one Q (a sayings source).

This latter hypothetical work consists of about 230 verses and is found in both Luke and Matthew. John's Gospel, which many see as being the final one of the four to be written, nonetheless appears to contain material from an earlier period. For example, there is detailed knowledge of Jerusalem prior to the destruction of AD 70 which obliterated most of the city and its traditional landmarks. There is also an intimate grasp of the topography of Israel. Therefore, even if we accept a late date for the composition or final editing of the book somewhere outside of Israel, it would still seem that the author was able to draw on local sources from an earlier date.

It is generally accepted within scholarship that Mark is the first account to be written and much of his work was subsequently incorporated and added to, by Matthew and Luke. What written or oral sources were available to the author of Mark we do not know. There is an early tradition within the Church that Mark was influenced by the preaching of the Apostle Peter. Now whatever, the truth behind this, if any, while Mark may have been the inheritor of disconnected homilies from the first followers of Jesus, he has certainly transformed these into the very vivid and dramatic account we have before us.

There is a realism in the diversity of the Gospel accounts, especially so when we begin to understand the processes which were behind their creation. The Gospels show great complementarity and cohesiveness despite their many and significant differences. They narrate the story of Jesus in a truly engaging way. A movie critic once said of *The Lord of the Rings* – 'It is an epic with grimy hands and a core of mystery.' These words perfectly describe the 'epic' of Jesus. If philosophy is the 'art of slow reading' (Nietzsche) then Gospel appreciation is most certainly that. Engaging, intriguing, compelling; the story captivates and challenges those with open hearts. Therefore, far from being a source of embarrassing problems that we have to try and get round, the Gospels furnish the faithful with an embarrassment of 'riches'. The Gospels are the Church explaining itself. It all goes back to Jesus: he and he alone, constitutes the primary cause and the foundational source for the Church's very existence.

Therefore, whatever the fruits of historical criticism of the Gospels, and there are many, it is at the holistic level of the Gospels as narratives, as 'story', that we ultimately have to engage. As already stated, the discipline of New Testament Studies is vibrant and stimulating as an academic enterprise. Historical criticism has brought many wonderful insights that have to be taken on board, raised many questions that cannot be ignored, and posed many challenges which have to be faced. But once the spotlight methods of 'form', 'source', 'redaction', and 'tradition' criticisms have done their forensic and investigative work, we are still left with the Gospels as literary and theological narratives in all their grandeur and universality. The explanation of the story they tell collectively, what forces generated it, what it meant then and what it means now, is an ongoing process and always will be. No book has been so dissected the past two centuries than the New Testament. Few figures in history has been so analysed and investigated as the Nazarene during the same period. Yet the enduring appeal of both book and person remains.

It is remarkable to think that one of the earliest, simplest yet most profound credal statements in the New Testament, is probably the affirmation that 'Jesus is Lord' (Paul's letters e.g. Romans 10:9). This tells us two things. First, that Jesus has a very important status for Christians. Second, this 'Lordship' is perceived of in present tense terms. For Christians, Jesus is not just viewed as an important figure in the past now dead, but an important figure for us today: a 'living' reality in the present. The key to understanding this of course, is the Christian belief in the Resurrection. This doctrine has been interpreted literally, spiritually and symbolically, and all three positions have their proponents today. The difficulty we have in establishing what really happened that first Easter lies both in the nature of the Gospel literature itself, and of course, our inability to get 'behind' the texts to the facts of the case. Perhaps a modern incident can highlight some of the issues for us.

During the Gulf War of 1991, an eight man British Army SAS patrol, code-named Bravo 20, went out on a mission deep behind Iraqi lines. What followed has become the subject of fierce controversy. Apparently, epitomising 'glorious failure' and incredible heroism against all the odds, this mission has become one of the most scrutinised and debated episodes in recent British military history. Starting with the patrol leader Andy McNab's best-selling account, we now have, at least five books on the subject. Three of these are written by patrol members, one by the SAS Regimental Sergeant Major at the time Peter Radcliffe, and one by Michael Asher a former soldier, explorer and fluent Arabic speaker who tried to trace the steps of the patrol, interview Arab witnesses and discover what 'really happened'. This last work was televised as a documentary. McNab's work was also made into a film. Amidst claim and counter claim (the patrol members do not agree with one another), there have been accusations of High Command betrayal, patrol incompetence, and allegations of a major fabrication. There have been civil court cases and extensive news coverage. If in this modern age of investigative journalism, intensive media operations and television documentaries, we still are unsure about the 'real truth' behind a much publicised incident in living memory where many of the participants are still alive and vocal, what chance do we have in reconstructing alleged incidents and events from ancient history?

Yet historical perspectives, and the beliefs or convictions that arise from them, are at the heart of ideological, social, cultural and political identities; they are instrumental in the founding and sustaining of nations and civilisations throughout time. History matters.

So where do we go from here in relation to the Resurrection of Jesus? Well at the risk of sounding lame and tame, whilst we may not be able to ascertain exactly *what* happened, we are left with the dilemma and puzzle that *something* happened. The founder died but the movement lived on affirming certain things about him and about the events of Easter. The question is not only what happened but why did the disciples of Jesus believe what they did?

Any open-minded reader of the New Testament writings can sense the excitement, the passion and the joy which pervades this material. There is a sense of triumph and celebration which is unmistakable. It is almost as though someone has just won the lottery jackpot! Paul exudes it, the book of Acts depicts it, and the Gospels have it through the warp and woof of their structure. It has long been said that Mark's account, the simplest and most basic of the Gospel narratives, is like a story told by a 'breathless schoolboy'. On the other hand, it is easy to detect echoes of doubt emerging between the lines. New Testament literature has often been described as 'tension-laden' and that is so true. There is a genuine sense that the writers are trying to articulate what is difficult to put into words. This is an experience which cannot easily be dismissed *or* explained. It is impossible here to be neat and tidy, to smooth out the rough edges and tie up the loose ends. This is an event which needs to be wrestled with and meaning wrought from it. It seems clear to me, that only a genuine conviction that somehow, and in some way, Jesus transcended death, can explain the characteristics of early Christianity.

Consider the following: a radical change of worldview; the change of holy day from Saturday to Sunday; no cult of worship at the tomb of Jesus; no practices of offering sacrifices; the preaching of the oxymoronic message of a crucified Messiah – which was both foolish and offensive in equal measure to those who heard it; the reorganisation of life and faith around the birth of hope fulfilled in Christ which so energised and impelled early Christian mission and evangelism. All of the above make sense only if understood in the light of the affirmation that 'Christ is Risen'.

That a powerful experience lay behind this conviction would seem to be reasonable and logical. Whether we understand that experience as having a natural or supernatural explanation is a moot point. The documents of the New Testament pulsate and resonate with the Easter message. Belief in the Resurrection of Jesus colours everything, pervades everything, shapes everything, and drives everything. Without it, would we even have heard of Jesus of Nazareth or the Sermon on the Mount, or the Parable of the Sower or the stories of the Prodigal Son and the Good Samaritan? It cannot be stressed enough, that at no time did the early followers of Jesus consider him as no more than a great teacher who died a martyr's death but who has left his teaching as a legacy to us. This perhaps is this most serious flaw in the methodology of the quest for the so called 'historical' Jesus.

Metaphorically speaking, the Resurrection is a like a plug in a sink. Pull out the plug and all the water drains away. Remove the Resurrection from the New Testament and everything evaporates. Or, changing the metaphor, the Resurrection is the keystone in an arch. It holds everything together. Remove it and the edifice collapses. As already stated, the Gospels were written from within a faith community for that faith community. We can categorise the process underlying this through the rubrics of experience, interpretation and proclamation. In and through Jesus, his followers believed that they had encountered the Divine. This in turn led to many experiences both individual and corporate, which were reflected on and interpreted within that community. Finally, an expression of this interpreted experience was given in the proclamation and preaching of the early Church and, subsequently, in the writings of the New Testament. Inherent in that message is both an affirmation that 'Jesus is Lord' (by virtue of the Resurrection however understood) and, an invitation to others to participate in this ongoing Christian experience.

For Christians it has always been more of a 'who' question than a 'what' and a 'how'. It is not that somebody, somewhere, sometime, somehow, had a post-mortem experience by being raised from death, but it is more that *this particular* person, Jesus of Nazareth, was raised from death. The Resurrection is not just a weird context-less anomaly but an essential element in a grand narrative. Without Jesus, the Resurrection does not make sense. Without the Resurrection, the story of Jesus doesn't make sense. That is why reductionist accounts of the 'Jesus of history' fail spectacularly and are usually quite banal, pale and empty, making absolutely zero impact. Put simply, if the church misunderstood Jesus then he is lost: and no amount of historical reconstruction, however sophisticated, will retrieve him. Therefore the traditional story lives on and we follow on with it.

It has been said that one of the triumphs of the Enlightenment was to ground truth claims in empirically verifiable evidence. Sounds reasonable, but what does it mean in practice? Over, the last two centuries, historical research has often been used to discredit the Christian religion, with many scholars asserting that the truth about the *real* Jesus who lived in 1st century Galilee/Judea can be reconstructed with a fair degree of plausibility through scientific principles. There are two major problems here. History is about judging possibilities and probabilities, often in the midst of competing claims and the paucity, ambiguity or contradictory nature of the evidence. Historical reconstructions, especially of ancient history are always fragile and provisional. Secondly, as already argued, the nature of the New Testament documents does not lend itself to this enterprise as much as we would like.

Historical research is a necessary, unstoppable, irresistible, fascinating and informative endeavour. It has a very important role to play in human thought and education but it has its limitations. Most perspectives in history are contested and they most certainly need qualification. This puts considerable constraints on those who would wish to use history for, or against, the Christian faith. Christian apologists for example, may want to argue that for every effect we need a sufficient cause. If anything approximating to the claims Christians make about Easter actually happened, this would help explain and justify the rise and success of the Christian movement. They may also want to point out what they see as deficiencies in secular counter-explanations. The problem is that *argumentation* (no matter how sophisticated or compelling one may find it) is not *demonstration*.

Historical events are, by nature one-off and unrepeatable. We accept their veracity on the basis of the testimony of others both oral and written, reinforced by other seemingly corroborating evidence. Where issues are contested, we often make judgments based on the plausibility of the arguments. This, despite claims to the contrary, is always a subjective affair. What else could it be? That fact does not mean that everything is relativized and we can never know truth, it is just to be honest and open about the limitations of the human condition and the constraints and qualifications that need to be placed on our epistemologies. As the late Jacob Bronowski said during his famous *Ascent of Man* documentary in the 1970s, 'We do not have a God's eye view of reality.' That certainly is true, not just of Cosmology or Physics; it is most certainly true of all historical reconstructions. So where does this leave us? To answer this, we need to return to the nature of the New Testament documents themselves. A.N. Wilson writes:

> *Anyone so ignorant, or so innocent, as to open the New Testament in the hope of finding a neutral historical source will be knocked back by a hurricane. Open it, and you will find a Pandora's box of personal challenges and ethical commands. By the end, the last thing you are worrying about is whether it is true, because you yourself have become a character in the story.*[22]

---

22 A.N. Wilson, *Jesus,* Sinclair-Stevenson 1992, p. 67.

I can confirm Wilson's observations in my own personal experience. When the Christian story so impacts us, literally capturing our hearts and imaginations so that we are drawn irresistibly into the drama itself, then *the* story becomes *our* story. This experience can then become the starting point of an adventure of faith which continually enriches and informs our personal lives.

Of course, in tandem with this comes a burning desire to know if this experience has any rational basis. The Church has always believed that the story of Jesus found in the canonical Gospels is rooted in historical reality (although to what extent will always be contested and debated) and, is constructed imaginatively and artistically from the interpreted experience of his followers. That construction contains both a proclamation and an invitation. Therefore, the authority of the Gospels resides not in them being infallible and inerrant documents, but rather, in their power to 'remake' the world for us.[23] They may not be in a literal sense the 'Word of God' but they become that for us when they 'grasp' us and we in turn 'grasp them'.

When I engage with the Gospels, I hear the words of Jesus through the affirmations and experiences of the early Christian community through which, and for which, the Gospels came to be. I claim to be a Christian for these words have so impacted my life and experience that I cannot be defined or understood apart from them. They have challenged my intellect, captured my imagination and shaped my life's work. I cannot prove the truth of these affirmations and experiences: I can only, like the first Christians share my story and live my life in the light of this.

I do not know, Douglas, whether any of the above argumentation has resonated with you or encouraged you to reflect further on specific issues. But I do hope, at the very least, that I have shown there is more to this subject than our contemporary 'cultured despisers' of Christianity allow for.

---

23 L.T. Johnson, op. cit. p. 168.

Chapter 4

The Voice of God!

In the O'Reilly interview already cited above, you also mentioned that you would probably need to hear a 'voice' in order to become a 'believer'. Be careful what you wish for Douglas! More decades ago than I care to mention, I was a young Police Constable working on a nightshift when challenged about my Christian faith by an older senior colleague. After a long interesting discussion he said that although I had put up a reasonable defence, he would really need to hear a voice or 'something' (the latter term wasn't specified) to turn him into a Christian.

My immediate response was to challenge him as to whether that was true. I asked him about this scenario: he is heading home in the dark after his shift and he suddenly had to stop the car due to a blinding light. At the same time a loud clear voice bellows out identifying as God. He is told that the Divine had listened to our conversation earlier and thought he would pay a wee visit. In response to this, I asked, would he excitedly wake up his wife to tell her when he got home? Would he phone me immediately to let me know what had happened? Would he share this amazing event with all our colleagues in the days that followed down at the Police Station? Would he contact the media? I didn't think so! Besides, what was he going to tell the psychologist when the Police Force recommended therapy sessions? Or more appositely, how would a psychologist decipher this story? I think I have a good idea what that would consist of. What would you tell your *Spectator* colleagues Douglas, if something similar was to happen to you? Of course such an event could be interpreted as an encounter with Aliens and not God but that's another story.

One of my favourite movies is *Wholly Moses!* (1980) starring the late Dudley Moore. It is a satire on the life of the great Jewish Prophet. The main character called Herschel is an idol-maker who one day overhears God's voice to a hidden-from-sight Moses on Mount Sinai. Thinking that the 'voice' is addressing him, Herschel sets off to rescue the people of Israel from Egypt. Unfortunately, at every stage of the adventure the character of Moses appears taking all the credit for what is happening. Believe me Douglas, there have been many times over the years when I think that my 'call' to ministry was actually to someone else and I misheard (although no literal voice was involved). It is a sobering thought!

Now I grant that there are miracles in the Bible and stories of alleged encounters between God and humans. What often goes unnoticed is how infrequent these are. The Scriptures are not full of supernatural occurrences and manifestations. They are an exception not a rule. They tend to be clustered around Moses and Jesus, not surprisingly, as in the storyline this represents the establishment of two respective Covenants. Outside of this, they are sparsely distributed. The same seems true of both Jewish and Christian history. Yes there are stories of the experiences of certain sages and saints in both traditions, but I would guess that the overwhelming majority of adherents of those two great faiths have never ever heard 'voices' or witnessed 'signs'.

Of course, this raises the issue of the Biblical events themselves. I have already acknowledged that, for example, in the case of the Resurrection there is a whole spectrum of interpretations of this within the Christian community and there always will be. The same is true of miracles, voices, dreams and other assorted phenomena contained in the Biblical narrative. Given the restrictions of this short work I cannot go into further detail on this important issue. That would have to be explored at another time. Instead, I want to concentrate on personal issues. I have never heard a literal 'voice' in relation to my faith nor witnessed or experienced a 'miracle' as normally understood. I don't know what I would think if I ever did? Rather than be inspired and overjoyed I think I would be puzzled and not a little disturbed. But then again, so were the Bible characters. On the other hand, to those who are receptive to it the world and our experience of it can be wonderfully illuminating and revelatory. I think it was Einstein who said, 'There are two ways to live your life. One is to see nothing as miraculous and the other is to see everything as miraculous.' I guess that is how I approach things.

I am fortunate to live in the majestic beauty of the Scottish Highlands and consciously breathe it in every day. I also love the Jewish toast *lechaim* (to life!) which, beyond the simple act of eating a meal, can often indicate an attitude of gratitude to the sheer 'givenness' and indeed 'gift' of self-conscious existence. Furthermore, as I have already indicated, I am deeply moved and engaged by the story of the Nazarene. During lockdown I recorded daily reflections for my congregation. One week the theme was 'Still Christian After All These years' which, as you might already have guessed, was a play on the title of the popular Paul Simon song 'Still Crazy After All These Years.' In today's world, being Christian and being crazy go together in the thinking of many. I would agree, but put a positive and rebellious spin on the latter term. Simon's song about a chance encounter with an old lover and a time of reminiscence over a couple of beers is beautifully written. It powerfully conveys a touch of wistfulness, melancholy, honesty, realism, gratitude and hope: a deeply moving and evocative combination. Whether it was autobiographical or just imaginative I don't know, but it touches a cord in me.

The feelings conveyed in the song metaphorically mirror and match my own experience of faith. If I was to meet a longstanding Christian friend over coffee and we were to reflect on how it all started for us and how we got to be where we are now, then I think the six terms I used above to describe the song would be very much part and parcel of our contemporary Christian journey. The 'voice' of Jesus mediated through the Gospel narratives was the one I responded to at the age of eighteen. Forty seven years later, through all the twists and turns of life and faith it is still the 'voice'

I respond to. I decided to follow Jesus then, and I continue to choose (and a choice it certainly is) to follow him now. Although, wiser, more experienced, more knowledgeable, more cynical and, at times, even more doubting, I continue on this pilgrimage.

There is a wonderful verse in John's Gospel where, after many people leave Jesus because the teaching is too hard, he addresses the twelve and asks if they too want to leave. It is Peter (of course!) who replies, 'To whom would we go? You have the words of eternal life. We believe and know that you are the Holy One of God' (John 6: 68, 69). As always for the Christian it is the 'who' question which comes before the 'what' and the 'how'. To appropriate biblical imagery I am often in my small boat in the middle of the squalls of life and surrounded by the fog of doubt. Then, periodically, the wind calms, the mists clear and there He is; the Nazarene, calling me from the shore. So far I've continued to steer in his direction. I would like to think I always will, but then again, who knows?

Continuing with the theme of 'voices' there is an enigmatic story from the Hebrew Bible which may be illuminating. The Prophet Elijah, one of the great Biblical figures, is on the run for his life from King Ahab and his wife Jezebel, and comes to Mount Horeb (the other name for Mount Sinai). It is here that he experiences an encounter with Yahweh the God of Israel. However, although the story details the phenomena of wind, earthquake and fire, the reader is told that God was not in any of these. After that there is a 'still small voice', or, as some translations put it, 'a gentle whisper', or even, 'the sound of silence' (1 Kings 19:12).

This is an intriguing story. The setting is the very place where Moses experienced the burning bush and the voice of God commissioning him for service. It is also the place where, later, the people of Israel were given the Law (Ten Commandments – Exodus 20) after the sound and fury of a theophany (Exodus 19: 16-19). Therefore, the apparent contrast with Elijah is quite striking. We are *explicitly* told that God is *not* in the natural phenomenon which Elijah observes. However, we are not told that he is definitely in the 'still small voice.' This is only hinted at.

The Hebrew phrase consists of three words and literally means a *voice* or *sound*, of *fine* or *thin*, *silence* or *quietness*. In our culture we talk of a silence so vivid we could 'hear a pin drop'. The same idea is possibly being presented here. In which case are we entering a realm of experience common and universal in religious practice? If this is true then the Elijah story may be moving the reader on from the dramatic days of Moses in the past, a past to which Elijah could not return (and neither can we) to a contemporary and less supernatural and miraculous engagement with the Divine. Prior to this, Elijah had witnessed the miracle on Mount Carmel before the prophets of Baal which had only led to him fleeing for his life in the next chapter. It seems that even powerful demonstrations of supernatural power have limited efficacy and don't always lead to positive outcomes for God or his servants!

Then again, some would argue that there was no past Golden Age of revelation and that these stories should never have been taken literally in the first place. They contain imaginative rhetoric and imagery to convey in literary form the intensity and importance of human encounter with, and experience of, the Divine.

Alternatively, assuming for example, that there was an historical Moses (as our Jewish friends would say, 'Maybe Moses didn't exist but he must have had a cousin!') did he see a literal burning bush and hear a literal voice? If we were standing beside the great man would we have seen and heard anything or was this vision internal to Moses? Or on the night of Jesus' birth when the angels were singing did some of the neighbour's poke their heads of their windows and complain 'who on earth is making such a racket at 3 o'clock in the morning!' Or, are we talking about visions or, as noted above, literary imagination here?

Of course none of this helps you very much Douglas because you lose out either way. If miracles are a thing of the past only used to establish the faith, or, if the texts themselves can be deconstructed as above, then you are not likely to hear a 'voice' anytime soon, unless of course, you have had too much wine! Now, I know that some of my more conservative brethren may want to tread some kind of middle path here. Yes, generally speaking, God's powerful interactions were originally to bring both the people of Israel and then subsequently, the Church into existence, but He can still, on occasion, do extra-ordinary things today according to his will and purpose. Perhaps that is the case. All I can say is that I personally have not been on the receiving end of such phenomena.

But as I have already indicated, how would hearing a voice affect you? Let me challenge you by saying if you fail to discern the 'voice' of Jesus in the Gospel accounts what makes you think that some out-of-the-ordinary experience will do the trick? May it not be the case that such an encounter would raise more questions than provide answers?

I was reminded of this recently by something I read by the New Testament scholar N.T. Wright, concerning the wonderful 1981 Film *Chariots of Fire*. This is a story about two star athletes Harold Abrahams and Eric liddell, one a Jew and the other a devout Christian. It is a fascinating portrayal of their respective lives and experiences at the 1924 Paris Olympics. One very revealing incident in the story is at the homecoming. Having won the gold medal in the 100yds, Abrahams is the last to get off the train at Waterloo Station and only after everyone else has gone. We are left with the impression that his delay was deliberate. It was a poignant anti-climax to the triumph and elation of that wonderful moment of crossing the finishing line in Paris. What was he going to do now? It was a return to the hum-drum of normal everyday life.

There is a story in the Gospels of the transfiguration of Jesus on the mountain top in the presence of the figures of Moses and Elijah. Peter as usual gets it wrong. He wants to build three shelters and the biblical aside is that 'he didn't know what he was saying' (Luke 9: 28-36). Peter didn't understand that these 'moments' when and if they happen, may be revealing and inspiring but also fleeting and transient. We can't stay on the mountain top for ever. We always return to the mundane lowland experiences which make up our everyday lives. For the pilgrim there may well be 'moments' of revelation, grace and blessing at some points on the way but mostly it is a case of putting one foot in front of the other and continuing the journey. Besides, there will always be nagging doubts that never completely evaporate about the nature, reality and veracity of these 'moments' should they occur.

Of course Douglas, should such an experience ever happen to you, have you not made it impossible for your atheist friends to be convinced by this as it will all be dismissed as a deep psychological need and a personal longing within you. You have, after all, publically declared that is what you are looking for!

Finally, let me refer again to my own story.

I have lived in the shadow of the Galilean all my life whether passively and culturally or consciously and committedly. Having been brought up in a nominal Christian environment, I, like many of my generation, attended Sunday school and then Boy's Brigade Bible class in the Sixties but left as soon as I was old enough to do so as this represented my parents' interests and not mine. It wasn't until many years later I had an 'evangelical' encounter through a friend at college and began my Christian journey as an adult. This was a genuine *Gestalt* moment when the background really did become foreground and perspective was radically altered. For the first time I understood that the Church had a 'beating heart' deep within the institutional structures. It was a 'hidden secret' so to speak, that even many Church members didn't seem to understand or know about.

Like most converts to the cause, I had a mix of abounding passion and enthusiasm alongside a hunger and thirst to know more. The lifeless and dull religious institution that was the Christian Church seemed a million miles away from the dynamic story of Jesus and his early followers as portrayed in the New Testament. That experience was a watershed for me. It has defined my life's journey ever since. Cynics often say that if you are not a socialist by the age of 20, you don't have a heart. However, if you are still a socialist by the age of 40, you don't have a brain. Many people would see a parallel here with religion. The movement, over time, from passionate fervour to sober moderation is all too common within Church circles and I can identify with some of that. Nonetheless I still have an evangelical 'heart' which I hope shines through what I write and communicate.

My journey has had many twists and turns over the years. I have moved through experience and intensive academic study from that initially simple, but powerful understanding of the Christian faith, to a more nuanced and informed position. Yet I cannot completely disown that dramatic starting point. Without it, my life would have taken a very different road and I would have missed out on what I consider to have been an amazing journey.

Whatever the validity of the truth-claims of the Christian faith and however arrogant they may appear to others, the faith I discovered all those years ago has had an incredibly positive and productive effect on me. Through this I was able to embrace life with its many contradictions and complexities. Inheriting the Grand Narrative that is the Christian Story, I developed an expansive vision of reality. What had been parochial became universal. What had been black and white was now filled with colour. What had been dull and lifeless was filled with momentum and vigour.

Emerging within this process was a very personal sense of identity, purpose and calling. Because of this, I became interested not only in Biblical studies and theology, but also history, archaeology, philosophy, science, politics and ethics. It began a life-long journey of personal development, academic education, and service to others. Not only has my mind been thrilled and broadened along the way but my heart has been deeply moved by the privilege granted to the clergy of being alongside others in the triumphs and tragedies and the laughter and tears of human existence. It could all have been very different. In saying 'Yes' to Jesus I discovered I was saying 'Yes' to life. So at a very personal level, I owe a huge debt of gratitude to the Christian tradition of which I have been a part. Therefore, despite the many challenges modernity poses for the Christian Faith, and these are considerable indeed, I am, 'still standing', to quote Elton John.

The institutional Church in its various forms has preserved the Christian faith down the ages but has often managed to do a great job of hiding its Saviour and keeping secret the power of his Gospel. Or, in some cases totally reversing what he stood for. It was Nietzsche (who else!) who famously said, 'The only true Christian died on the cross.' That theme is also echoed in an anonymous quotation I came across many years ago: 'Christ was crucified in the east and buried in the West.'

Yet the Nazarene still 'lives' and his words and presence have the power to challenge and change even the hardest of hearts and the most wayward of lives. As he himself once said, 'Let those who have ears hear.' (Matthew 13:9) It is down to each individual how they respond to that.

Chapter 5

Future Orientation – 'Still Dreaming Christian Dreams'

The subtitle which you will recognise, refers to a quote from Don Cupitt which you have utilised and seemed to concur with.[24] Despite Europe losing its foundational story the 'debris' is, for you, all around us but we don't realise its significance. Nonetheless, whether we know it or not the dreams we may have for the future are still influenced by that Christian legacy. This begs the question as to what exactly our dreams are, or could or should be.

Your last two books – *The Madness of Crowds* and *The Strange Death of Europe* are truly wonderful. I won't try to add to the multitude of accolades that have already been given except to say that they are the best works I have read for a long time and so badly needed in these strange, challenging and disturbing times. I can only hope (and pray!) that they will be as influential as they deserve to be. I was pleased that you acknowledged the positive role Christianity has played in European history and culture. Your view of European history as an interacting triad of Greco-Roman tradition, Christian faith and Enlightenment thought, is spot on from my perspective and a very welcome change from the negative evaluation of many, but by no means all, contemporary atheists, humanists and secularists.[25]

It might also be added, that all three of these tributaries were not, and are not, unmitigated 'goods'. Christianity has had its dark side, so did Classical tradition, and we are selective in what we extol about the Enlightenment. Nonetheless, without this synthesis Europe would be a very different place. Although, as

24 Douglas Murray, *The Strange Death of Europe*, Bloomsbury 2018, p. 213.
25 *Ibid.*, p. 261.

your work reminds us, that is rapidly changing. I would also like to add that I prefer the term 'Judeo-Christian tradition' rather than just 'Christian'. We Christians, and indeed, Europeans, owe a lot to our Jewish brothers and sisters and that needs to be highlighted in this age of increasing supersessionism[26] on behalf of both Islam and Christianity which, in turn, often feeds into or unconsciously supports anti-Semitism. This often manifests itself in relation to the nation state of Israel of which, like you, I am a supporter and 'Friend'.

We seem to live at the sunset of European values and, as already noted above, the ebb-tide of Christian faith. The future, in the eyes of many, does not look bright. But history can be a powerful teacher and encourager as well as a source of pessimism and cynicism.

Historian Barbara Tuchman wrote of the passing of the 19th century as the ending of 'the most hope-filled, change filled, progressive, busiest and richest century the world had ever known.' However, with the death of Queen Victoria the sense of an era's end was palpable. Subsequently, with the retirement of Lord Salisbury at the conclusion of the Boer war, there was a vivid consciousness of a final conclusion to what had gone before. The French paper *Le Temps* of Paris wrote:

> *What closes today with lord Salisbury's departure is a whole historic era. It is ironic that what he hands on is a democratized, imperialized, colonialized and vulgarized England – everything that is antithetic to the Toryism, the aristocratic tradition and the High Church that he stood for. It is the England of Mr Chamberlain, not, despite his nominal leadership, of Mr Balfour.*[27]

This makes me smile. Just as every human being is a living, breathing contradiction, a manifestation of good and bad at the same time; so too, every period of history can be judged similarly. Humans

---

26 The belief that the Christian Church, or the Islamic *umma*, has replaced Israel.

27 Barbara Tuchman, *The Proud Tower*, Macmillan Press 1983, pp. 58, 59.

like binary judgments. We make them all the time. How often throughout history have some lamented the end of a perceived golden or glorious age whilst others have rejoiced at its passing? Alternatively, how often have some heralded the dawning of a new age whilst others have remained pensive, sceptical, and concerned about the road being travelled? Has this scenario not played itself out at the changing of every era with all the contingencies of history and the paradoxes of human effort, expectations, dreams, disappointments and sobering realities all in play at the same time? Such is the waxing and waning, the flowing and ebbing of history.

Tuchman notes that the year before her death Queen Victoria had been returning from a trip to Ireland in her royal Yacht. In the midst of rough seas the boat was buffeted by a strong wave. The Queen sent word to the Captain that it 'must not occur again'. But, as Tuchman, with an eye to the unforeseen turmoil of the 20th century soon to begin in 1914, concludes, 'the waves would not stand still'.[28] They never do!

Of course, predicting the future is always a difficult activity as you yourself acknowledge. Could anyone living in 1900 have predicted how the 20th century would play out? Can we predict how this 21st century will develop and change? Will we see the total collapse of the nation state or its resurgence? Will the world be dominated again as it was before by great 'civilizational' states? Will democracy survive and in what form? Who knows? Predictions are easy but history is surprising.

With regard to immigration and religion will we see Islamic domination of Europe or will Christian immigration from the developing world renew and revive European Christianity? Will there be an Islamic reformation? Will there be a secular fightback to all this? Again who knows? All of these are, in their own way plausible possibilities and there are authors who argue for each of the above scenarios. Perhaps it will be a mix of all of them.

It is sobering to think that the high point for the churches in Britain was the 1950s (not the 1850s!). My own denomination,

---

28 *Ibid.*, p. 59.

the Church of Scotland, recorded its highest ever membership in 1956. Then came the cultural revolution in the 1960s and the rejection of Christianity for its out of date morals, its Establishment associations and of course, because it was the 'parents' faith'. It was also boring! Post-war prosperity was the wave that buoyed this transformation. Today, shopping malls are the new 'cathedrals' and retail therapy the new 'spirituality'. Sport, of all kinds, delivered at the touch of a button is the new 'worship', and reality TV the new 'mind off – smile on' escapism of the age. Christians are as caught up in this as anyone else. Religion at its core requires a lot of effort, commitment, and self-sacrifice, something which today is not that appealing! Who wants the hassle?

For so many in our society, it's not that they are opposed to religion, it's more the case that they're not interested; it's not on their radar at all. They get by just fine without it. Again, that too could change. Nothing is set in stone. A colleague told me recently of a conversation he had with a young lad of 17 who had just joined the Roman Catholic Church. When my clerical friend expressed surprise at this he was told, 'It's my Dad's generation who are atheists not mine.' I could add several more stories in the same vein but anecdotes do not make a trend. Nonetheless, a review of Christian history indicates the resilience of the faith. G.K. Chesterton once remarked that in history there were at least 'five times when it looked like Christianity was going to the dogs but in each case it was the dogs that died.' So where do we go from here?

I hope and trust that the strength of European tradition comprising the legacy of the best of Classical civilization, Christian faith and Enlightenment values will prove robust enough for the challenges that lie ahead. In 2006, the then Chief Rabbi of Britain, Sir Jonathan Sacks (subsequently Lord Sacks – sadly recently deceased) used an interesting illustration in an article in *The Times*.[29] The title of the article was – *The prophets are our unflappable sat-nav, not the lost car in front.* It is sprinkled with

---

29 *The Times*, February 4th 2006.

typical Jewish humour and insightfulness. Obviously enthralled by his latest gadget and its calm authoritative voice and endless patience in reconfiguring routes for stupid drivers he writes, 'From this machine I have learned one of the great lessons in life. However, many wrong turns you may have taken, if you know where you want to be, there is a route from here to there. If that isn't a source of hope, what is?'

In contrast, he references the story told by the American naturalist William Beebe who came across a huge moving circle of army ants in the jungle of Guyana. They did this for two days before dying of exhaustion/starvation. The reason seems to be that when a group of ants are separated from the colony they simply follow the one in front. This is fine assuming the one in front knows where it is going. If not, the consequences can be severe. Ironically Douglas, that story is told in James Surowecki's book *The Wisdom of Crowds*. It surely would have been more appropriate to your own *Madness of Crowds*! For Sacks, the fate of the ants may be a metaphor for the 'march of human folly'. In contrast, it is the voice of all prophets down through the ages (not just biblical ones) who have often called into question the direction of travel of their people, societies and nations. We are back again to 'voices'. Douglas, hope you are listening!

Of course, in many ways you yourself have been, and are a much needed prophetic voice in our day and age and long may that continue. However, to avoid being no more than a 'voice crying in the wilderness', to appropriate a biblical expression, your message needs not just to be heard but embodied by others in some form or other. In other words it needs a community. I do not mean anything formal and structured, as in a new organisation or such like, but only the communication and cooperation of like-minded and concerned individuals who will be found in various sections of our society from religionists to humanists. I remember in the 1970s a book by Michael Griffiths entitled *Cinderella with Amnesia*. It is now a classic, with a message for the churches which is more important than ever. The metaphor is of the contemporary church being like Cinderella sitting in the ashes having forgotten who she is, where she came from, and what she could be. Can we extend the metaphor to include European societies in the light of your penetrating critique?

In our society we are familiar with an act of Remembrance for the War dead once a year. We are always told that we should 'never forget' and that is right. But we have forgotten in so many ways the struggles and sacrifices that have made our nation and the continent of Europe what it is. It is far from being perfect and its history is an ambiguous and tarnished one. Nonetheless we enjoy great freedoms here which not only cannot be taken for granted but which are, as history abundantly demonstrates, always vulnerable and fragile. It is imperative in our contemporary situation that we remind ourselves *who* we are and *why* we are. The long retreat must be stopped; the aimless drift must be corrected; the self-flagellation and self-deprecation expressed in many quarters must cease. A recovery of a realistic, honest, and balanced pride in our roots and in what we have become will be not only a healthy, but an essential, counterbalance to much of the negativity that abounds.

I believe that in any process regarding the renewal of European culture the Christian churches could, and should, have a role to play but given their current decline, loss of identity, and demographic deficit, that prospect is becoming increasingly difficult to envisage. However, it is not impossible. Of course, any involvement from the churches even if they were strong enough, could only be as a partner not as a controlling or dominant voice. History demonstrates that religion and power, or religion and politics, are poor bedfellows. It was Max Weber who distinguished between charismatics and bureaucrats in the origin and development of religion. The former are the prophets and poets who inspire others and usually represent the founders or reformers of faith. The latter are the consolidators and organisers whose orbit is around questions of power, authority and control. This is where the 'dark side' of religion is usually manifested. There is an Italian proverb which states, 'No river rises with pure water.' That is true of all revolutions, reformations and radical social and political upheavals and changes. It is certainly true of the history of religion. Taken to extremes every ideal can become demonic and every virtue a vice. Therefore checks and balances are always required.

So, given that the Churches may be slow and ineffectual in engaging seriously with this project what else can be done? Well I'm not a social thinker or revolutionary so I am as perplexed as the next person about the way forward. Perhaps this is where your friend Richard Dawkins comes in with his idea of memes. The memes from the triad of tributaries noted above which have shaped and moulded Western Europe are around us, among us, and within us. Perhaps they need to be identified, unified, personalised and promoted. This can only happen through conversation and engagement.

Over the years I have spoken with and publicly debated Humanists and Atheists and found that alongside our serious differences there are many areas of agreement. In fact, when I first read the 2002 Amsterdam Declaration which is, I'm led to believe, the official defining statement of World Humanism, I was surprised to discover that I could sign up to all 7 Fundamentals. Now maybe that says more about me than the declaration, but there it is! Conscious of the allegations of 'turf wars' over words like 'humanism', I still think that in some way 'hyphenated-humanism' is an umbrella term under which religionists and secularists can meet in the future. I have just bought a book by Peter Boghossian and James Lindsay entitled *How to Have Impossible Conversations* (Lifelong Books 2019). It is a manual for engaging those who are diametrically opposed to you in what they believe and stand for and how to have a civil conversation with them. It is packed with wisdom, insight and practical techniques. A much needed work for our divided and fractures societies. I predict this book will be a major text in the future for everyone who wants to promote a better society.

Of course, if there are *impossible* conversations, there are by inference, *possible* ones. Have we tried hard enough to initiate the latter far less exhaust them? I don't think we have. For example, the Churches need to discuss seriously the subject of the Nation State and uphold its value especially post Brexit: something I fear which many Church representatives will find hard to do. Christians and Humanists as well as having debates around science/religion and whether God exists or not should also have constructive dialogue about a way forward for our society so that freedom of conscience and freedom of speech continue to be vigorously upheld. By the way, can I say in passing, that as a subscriber to the *New Humanist* Magazine (I like to keep tabs on what they are getting up to!) that I value its distinct lack of polemic and broad minded take on a whole range of issues. Let's hope the 'New Atheist' bubble has burst.

Regarding *impossible* conversations I guess dialogue between Christianity and Islam would come under that category. This would need to be a sharing of the fears, worries, concerns and hopes of each community. How do we see each other? Is there a real chance of genuine understanding of the other? As far as I can see there isn't at the moment. These conversations need to be brave, honest, real, and dare I say it, robust. There are very important issues around persecution, blasphemy, apostasy, misrepresentation, freedom of conscience and freedom of speech that need to be aired. All of this ties into a vision for the future of Europe in general and Britain in particular.

I am sure you would agree Douglas, that alongside the secularist denial of any positive Christian influence in British and European history, there are, it seems, some Christians who want to denounce and disown that same legacy; an issue very much to the forefront of our minds as a result of the Black Lives Matter movement. I have already stated that the Christian legacy is a mixed bag of good and bad, as is British and European history. But as a 'host' nation of a 'host' continent which has traditionally been a safe haven for immigrants and refugees, we should have, at the very least, some expectations of those who find a home here. But then, that requires us to think long and hard not only about who and what we are but also how we became what we are. On that foundation we can build who and what we can become in the future. On the bright side we must have, as a nation, got something right if many people still want citizenship in our country. Nonetheless, in the face of negative and increasingly strident voices, we will certainly have our work cut out to make the case.

One final thought to ponder. I have just read an article by Matthew Paris in the Spectator entitled – *Are liberal conservatives now history?* His concluding paragraph caught my eye:

> *We almost thought we were forerunners. Now I almost feel we're remnants. When does a forerunner become a remnant, and how does it know?*[30]

Does that sentiment apply here I wonder, albeit in a very different context? Will the tide turn in the struggle to save, nurture and build on the best of European and British values or is it a vain rear-guard action that is being fought by a remnant? Of course, biblically speaking, God has often used 'remnants' time and time again to great effect. Perhaps that will be the case again. Time will tell!

---

30 *Spectator Magazine*, 5th September 2020.

Chapter 6

The Christ and his Kingdom: Changing Worldviews

In conclusion Douglas, I refer to a recent interview you did on YouTube entitled 'God Shaped Hole'. You reflected on our contemporary situation and characterised it as a move over time, from 'one belief system to another'. In this case, from a classical and dominant Christian culture to a secular 'rights' based one. This, you maintained, has had the effect of leaving a 'God shaped hole' in European society which hasn't yet been filled. Furthermore you indicated that the latter worldview owed far more to the former than was acknowledged far less understood. I found that perspective both interesting and challenging and sense that you and historian Tom Holland (who was also interviewed for the same channel) are, essentially, on the same ground here. Incidentally, like you he seems to be a 'prodigal' who may be in the process of 'returning home'. Therefore, in the light of that, let me return to the main theme again.

Consider the following. A tale of two Kings: one who was born in a royal household, the other, within a peasant community; one who was tutored by the philosopher Aristotle, the other by the religious tradition of the synagogue; one whose feet trod from the mountains of Macedonia to the plains of the Punjab, the other, never left the land of Israel; one whose Kingdom was established by the power of the sword, the other, by the power of his message; one whose Kingdom did not survive his death, the other's is still growing; one who died in Babylon in despair and frustration at his own mortality, the other who died in Jerusalem with the piercing cry 'My God, my God, why have you forsaken me?'; one who was called Alexander, the other, who was called Jesus.

This astonishing contrast is full of paradox and perplexity and raises many questions for us. Of course, not all have been happy with the origin and success of Christianity. Nietzsche, who admired the heroic characters of Ancient Greece and Rome, viewed the Christian faith as originating in, and continuing to propagate, the flawed perspective of the downtrodden, the poor and the slave. A.C. Swinburne in his 1866 poem addressed to the Roman goddess Proserpina which laments the rise of Christianity and the displacement of paganism, has the now famous quotation, 'Thou hast conquered, O pale Galilean; the world has grown grey from your breath.' No doubt, this sentiment would have been shared by many in ancient Rome as it was during the Enlightenment, and, as it undoubtedly is in our contemporary world.

Nonetheless, the effect of that one solitary life and death of a first century Jewish peasant/rabbi/prophet/messiah in historical terms brings the complex issue of his identity and status into sharp focus. What kind of King was he? What kind of Kingdom are we talking about? The sign the Roman Governor placed above the head of Jesus at his execution read 'King of the Jews'. Why? What were his political motives for this and what were the pretentions, if any, of the man who was executed? I would love to know Douglas, what your response is to the contrast above and what your answers are to the questions raised by this.

Within the first twenty years of the church's existence (as the letters of Paul testify to) the terms *Jesus* and *Christ* became interchangeable. Yet one is a name and the other a title. Why and how did that happen? It would seem that the modern distinction between the Jesus of history and the Christ of faith was not a problem for the followers of Jesus. Is that a problem for you? If it is, and the problem is insurmountable, then nothing I have written will have made any difference, assuming of course, you read this far! On the other hand, if you are still open and questioning I hope that something that I have shared with you may help you continue the journey.

Some critics have expressed amazement that, as they see it, one of history's most radical visionaries (Jesus) could be replaced by one of the world's most reactionary institutions (the Church). But then, on serious reflection, could it have been otherwise? Has that process not happened to all religions? However religions begin, without community organisation, disciplined focus and strong leadership, faiths can come and go as quickly as shooting stars in space; as many have done throughout history. In a hostile world which can see the rapid dissipation of beliefs and the rapid dissolution of ideals in the challenging flux of life, new movements can only survive and promulgate by anchoring themselves in reality.

That process of social adaptation always involves pragmatic choices and rational compromises which can be objected to and criticised, especially by succeeding generations. But idealism and aspiration always need to be tempered by realism. The Jesus movement didn't die out in the hillsides of Galilee: it adapted to urban life and, subsequently, to Imperial favour; but not without changes and costs. Jesus, who had opposed the State with egalitarian, non-violent revolution, and who was brutally crushed by that State, became the Divine figure who was seen to bless and sanctify the State, using power and coercion to further his Kingdom on earth. As Andrew Marr said in a TV documentary on world history, 'Constantine replaced the Cross with a Sword!' James Bulloch writes candidly about that great Roman critic of Christianity, Celsus:

'What would happen if an emperor became a Christian?' Celsus asked in a prophetic moment. His implicit answer was that society would collapse. Certainly, society as the Roman world knew it would have collapsed: but when this very situation arose the consequences did not follow. Celsus had assumed that a Christian emperor would practise the commands of Christ as he saw the Church of his time doing. When the time came the Church found herself committed to a course of action contrary to all her past principles.[31]

---

31 James Bulloch, *Pilate to Constantine*, St Andrew Press 1981, p. 315.

But is this fair or realistic? Can we not understand why some, conscious of the experience of past persecution, saw Constantine's alleged conversion as a blessing? Or, why some, cognisant of the Church's universal mission, saw this event as a providential opportunity. Yes, it came with a price, it always does! But there could have been no growth or development from religious sect to established denomination to institutional Church within the ancient world in general, and the Roman Empire in particular, without a trade off in costs and benefits. That is the way life is and the way history works. Therefore we need not be too sanctimonious or judgemental here.

At the end of the day, the cynical actions of Constantine – the fact that his patronage of the Christian church appears to have been for his own political ends – is powerful testimony in itself to the already existing social and cultural influence of that church in the Roman world. How did that come about? In the light of historical experience it has been said that 'revolutions are dreamt up by thinkers and carried out by bandits': a comment that usually elicits a knowing smile from those who hear it.

But these sentiments hardly apply to the revolution that took place within the pagan world through early Christianity. David Bentley Hart argues that violent revolutions can often achieve sudden and dramatic change in the ordering of societies but usually do not have the means to transform cultures in the long term. They may radically alter the past but do not excel in creating a future. He writes:

> *The revolutions that genuinely alter human reality at the deepest levels – the only real revolutions, that is to say – are those that convert minds and wills, that reshape the imagination and reorient desire, that overthrow tyrannies within the soul. Christianity, in its first three centuries, was a revolution of this latter sort.*[32]

---

32 David Bentley Hart, *Atheist Delusions: The Christian Revolution and its Fashionable Enemies*, Yale University Press 2009, p. 183.

I remember being intrigued by a story about Menachem Begin the former Prime Minister of Israel. Grand preparations for his State funeral had to be cancelled, including the customary attendance of International dignitaries, when it was discovered that his wishes were for a simple religious ceremony at the graveside on the Mount of Olives where he was to be interred beside two of his former comrades who had committed suicide in prison before they were due to be executed by the British authorities for 'terrorist' acts in the 1940s. The man who famously rephrased Descartes for his own cause saying 'We fight therefore we are', was someone who had fought all his life, at various times being a 'wanted' man by the Nazis, the Russians and the British. He died still identifying with that cause and with his people after a lifetime of service.

Now whatever ethical reservations some people may have about Zionism, Irgun, and Begin's political views (and l know there are many who have them), it still is a powerful example of a lifelong and dedicated commitment to one's ideals. When I first heard this story I thought about a quote from William James: 'As life closes, all a man has done seems like one cry or sentence.' I often wonder what my cry or sentence will be? How will we each be remembered? How do we want to be remembered?

The great Protestant Reformer Martin Luther said, 'Every man must do two things alone; he must do his own believing and his own dying.' It is very easy to hide in a religious institution like a church especially one that seems to have lost its soul as appears to be the case in our national denominations in England and Scotland. I fully understand the attraction of the aesthetic side of church buildings/music/liturgy and have no complaint with those who enjoy this without feeling the need to be card carrying believers. But there is more, much, much, more. 'We're all mad here', said the Cat to Alice in Wonderland and that is what it must have felt like in the early church and also today in our modern world wherever Christians embrace in heart and mind the life transforming message of the Gospel. But then as the great wordsmith Nietzsche said, 'Those who were seen dancing were thought to be insane by those who could not hear the music.'

I have already made reference to Tom Holland; in a YouTube interview entitled 'A Secular Historian Loses his Faith in Liberalism' he acknowledges the 'power' of the Christian story. Having wrestled with this on what has been, for him, a surprising journey he now admits that he doesn't have it all worked out and pinned down, but finds himself 'surrendering' to this story. That image resonates with me at a deep level and I realise that even in my darkest moments of wrestling and doubt that is exactly what I have done on many an occasion. The Christian journey can only really begin with this openness.

The late T.F. Torrance, probably one of the finest theologians Scotland ever produced, was a past recipient of the Templeton prize for outstanding contributions to science and religion. He served as a padre in the Second World War. One day in Italy, he came across a young soldier who was mortally wounded. He asked Torrance, 'Is God really like Jesus?' The padre assured him that was the case. That was all that the soldier said and he died shortly after. That incident was to have a dramatic impact on the rest of Torrance's life and work, and in part, drove his creative and scholarly engagement with the Christian Faith. It certainly is a multi-million dollar question for all of us. But here is the sharp dividing line between those who think that such statements are vacuous nonsense and those who, at the very least, are curious to know if there is more to this.

Our Jewish brothers and sisters have a lovely greeting *G'mar tov* – 'finish well' (literally – 'A good finish') which is used at Yom Kippur and expresses the wish that the person be inscribed and sealed in the book of life for a good year. At a personal level, I want to take that sentiment in an expanded way and relate it in a Christian context to the words of the Apostle Paul – 'I have fought the good fight, I have finished the race, I have kept the faith' (2 Timothy 4:7). Despite my many problems with traditional

Christianity and institutional religion, I would like to be able to make a similar statement at the end of my life. I want to 'finish well'. I want my life to have counted for more than just questions and doubts. There is a saying, 'Doubt is a common experience of mankind but it can never be a way of life.' I want to move 'beyond doubt' not in the sense of denying its reality and even necessity; nor in trying to remove it or overcome it through a contrived certainty, but just in the sense of not allowing it to have the *last* word, or even the *only* word. Is that possible?

I believe it is, even for a troubled soul like me! How about you Douglas?

It will be apparent from many of the things I have already written above, that a term which helps to categorise me and qualify my religious faith is 'pilgrim'. Let me explain this further. Pilgrimage seems to be all the rage these days. Certainly in Scotland, ancient pilgrim routes are being opened and developed with the tourist industry realising there is a viable and developing market for this. Furthermore, old pilgrim routes are being opened up throughout Europe with the annual numbers at traditional sites increasing at an amazing rate e.g. the famous *Camino de Santiago* between France and Spain.

Pilgrims come in all forms: those wanting to deepen faith; those searching for connection; those open to new experiences or challenges; those just taking time out from the stress and noise of life; and those who are just curious. For me, pilgrimage is a metaphor for a spiritual journey that has two different directions. First, looking backwards in time to explore and engage historically and critically with the Faith tradition that I am part of; then second, looking forwards in time to explore the continuing relevance of this faith in a fast-moving and ever-changing world.

I am both a child of the Reformation and the Enlightenment. The roots of my life are in an ancient Faith but I live in the modern age with all its complexity, wonder and knowledge. That means, if I can appropriate another descriptive term, that I am very much an 'amphibian' inhabiting two different worlds. It is an appropriate and revealing metaphor. Biologically speaking, these two worlds cannot be inhabited simultaneously. At some point the sand meets the sea. On one side it is wet, and on the other it is dry. Therefore, the amphibian at any given time is either on the land or in the sea. Hence, speaking personally and existentially, the inherent tensions, struggles, paradoxes and mild 'schizophrenia' that characterises my contemporary pilgrim journey. There are siren voices which call me to abandon superstition and delusion and embrace materialism and atheism. That I cannot do. It wouldn't work anyway. If I am a contemporary Christian with doubts and difficulties, I would also be an atheist with exactly the same only worse.

Needless to say Douglas, every pilgrim needs resources for the journey. A map or guide book is always a good start. It has been said 'If you don't know where you are going then any road will take you there!' But not all paths lead up the mountain top. Some lead over the precipice. The Christian journey begins with, and is informed by, the creeds and confessions of the Church which are a guide to reading and interpreting the Scriptures. Without this governing pattern it is very easy to get lost. The New Testament can be understood as a series of confessional documents written in narrative or letter form which are foundational and indispensable for the Christian Church regarding its identity, destiny, mission and purpose. There are two issues here.

The first concerns the staggering claims of the New Testament texts. They are positively breath-taking in their scope. As already noted, they centre on the figure of Jesus of Nazareth as the 'Christ' of God. They claim not only a unique and unparalleled revelation of the Divine in and through him but also claim that what he accomplished in his death and resurrection has universal significance for the whole of creation. It is no surprise then that a scholar like N.T. Wright can argue that if Jesus was not the turning point of history then 'the Church is simply wasting its time.'[33]

---

33 N.T. Wright, *The Challenge of Jesus*, SPCK 2000, p. 15 and *Simply Christian*, SPCK 2006 pp. 78, 79.

Of course, in our contemporary culture such comments are bound to invite ridicule, annoyance, exasperation, or at the very least a wry smile and the shaking of heads. Yet this is the great dividing line in the Western world which cannot be ignored, bridged or fudged. The multi-million dollar question is what if the New Testament portrayal of Jesus is true? It changes everything does it not?

If we acknowledge that the Christian Church, overall, has had a positive influence in the shaping and the forming of the Western world, then that influence cannot be separated out from the worldview of Christianity.[34] At the heart of that worldview is the great affirmation of the 'Word made flesh' (John 1: 14). Take the Christ out of Christianity and you have an empty shell. De-divinise the Nazarene and the Church is a withered vine. Place Jesus on the same level alongside all the *other* religious teachers, prophets, gurus and wise men in history and you short circuit the 'power' of the Gospel.

This brings me to the second issue, namely the startling loss of faith within the contemporary Church. I made reference above to what I imagined to be the secular responses to N.T. Wright's assertion of Jesus as the 'turning point of history'. More concerning is the hunch that I have, based on personal experience, that many within the Church itself would react the same way. Organisations like the 'Progressive Christian Network' and 'Free to Believe' attract both lay members and clergy who cannot ascribe to the traditional creedal framework of the Christian Church, many of whom would deny that there is such a thing as 'Orthodoxy'. This was further highlighted for me in a recent episode of the BBC TV Sunday programme 'The Big Questions' hosted by Nicky Campbell. The discussion was entitled, 'Do we misunderstand Jesus?' (31st January 2021). I found it exasperating and mildly depressing to watch. If I was to sum up the gist of the focus it would be that Jesus,

---

34 For the influence of Christianity in history see Nick Spencer, *The Evolution of the West*, SPCK 2016, and Rodney Stark, *The Triumph of Christianity*, HarperCollins 2011.

though an ancient figure in history, taught some interesting and relevant things for us today in the 21st century. Unfortunately this has got covered over by supernatural and superstitious elements which are at best a major distraction and at worst a hindrance to understanding the 'real' Jesus. The culprit here is of course the Christian Church. Forgive me, but I find this all so 18th century![35]

Of course, no-one thought to mention that without the influence of the Christian Church on the West and the power of the Gospel stories, no-one in the modern world would be the least bit interested in a handful of sayings from a first century Galilean Jew abstracted from that. In fact, we would not even have any record of the teachings of Jesus without the Gospels and the Christian Church! Lastly, and more concerning for me, was the point made on a couple of occasions during the programme that many contemporary Christians share these views and were trying to creatively adapt their faith to the realism of the modern world.

None of this is surprising. Christianity has been on the defensive since the Enlightenment and a creeping secularism has extensively eroded the foundations of the Christian worldview. We live in the midst of this. The early Church Father Tertullian famously asked 'What has Athens to do with Jerusalem, the Academy with the Church?' A great question even if Tertullian meant it rhetorically. I feel very privileged to have been educated in the Academy (Athens) but I was then sent out to serve and work for the Church (Jerusalem) and was left, as an individual, to put the jigsaw pieces together and join the dots of that education all by myself. This explains the nature and substance of my own personal pilgrimage. My journey has taken me from a very conservative position when younger to the opposite end of the spectrum when older. In these recent years I have returned to a more central ground and am content to stand within the traditional creedal framework of the Christian faith. This has been both an intellectual

---

35 Famous figures who took this position included Thomas Jefferson and Benjamin Franklin.

and deeply emotional struggle. It is out of that experience that I write this work.

Many years ago I taught a course at Aberdeen University on secular approaches to faith. This examined the methodologies of anthropology, sociology, psychology, and philosophy in relation to the origin and understanding of religion. Many of the students were taken aback at what they considered the negativity and hostility of these disciplines towards the subject matter. I pointed out that in a University setting these approaches were valid. However, they tended to represent the 'outsider's' perspective ('etic' in sociological terminology) and in contrast I maintained that the 'insider's' perspective ('emic') was essential too. Theology was the discipline attuned to this dimension. Unfortunately we were not considering the insights of that discipline on the course. At University in the modern world it can feel that the 'citadel of faith is under siege and the walls are already breached' (the words of one of my former students). I can concur with that experience but have come full circle in my own pilgrimage. That is why the words of T.S. Eliot from the *Four Quartets* resonate so deeply with me.

> We shall not cease from exploration
>
> And the end of all our exploring
>
> Will be to arrive where we started
>
> And know the place for the first time.

Like the prodigal son I have come home and I now greatly appreciate and value beyond price the epic 'story' of Jesus of Nazareth that was bequeathed to the Church to preserve and transmit throughout history. I acknowledge with greater conviction than ever before the strength and enduring relevance of the Christian creed. I stand in gratitude for the witness of the great minds and honest hearts of those both scholarly and lay who have kept the candle of faith burning brightly on dark days and in testing times.

However Douglas, we live in an age where the religious and secular horizons concerning the evaluation of Christianity are dominated by the so called quest for the Historical Jesus and have been for some considerable time. This shows no sign of abating any time soon. At least from the 1980s it seems that every Christmas and Easter we are treated to a documentary on TV giving us the latest research by scholars on 'what really happened!' The fact that the perspectives on this keep changing over the years doesn't seem to bother anyone. Over the same time period the News Media have had countless reports and interviews with alleged controversial scholars and authors on the issue of Jesus and the Gospels. None of this ever argues for or defends the traditional Christian understanding of the person and work of Jesus. When we add the popularity and extended publicity of the Dan Brown novels and films, is it any wonder that much of the general public have a negative view of Christianity and many Church members are concerned and confused?

Despite the initial appearance of impressive erudition, the serious flaw in the whole enterprise of the Quest for the Historical Jesus is methodological. When the theological framework of the Gospels is dismantled, as it always is in this project, all that is left are a handful of 'jigsaw pieces' lying on the table removed from the 'picture' they were taken. These pieces are then reorganised and placed within another fabricated and imaginary picture 'painted' by historical theory and alleged insights from cross-cultural anthropology and sociology. The arbitrary and subjective nature of this enterprise does not lead to greater clarity only a multiplicity of competing and sometimes contradictory images which raise more questions than answers. Jesus was possibly an eschatological Prophet, a wandering Cynic, a charismatic Hasid, a political Revolutionary, a religious Reformer, a Zealot, an Essene, a Magician, a Gnostic Sage, a proto-Pharisee, a rogue Rabbi and even, a crypto-Buddhist.[36] Such varied and diverse portraits cannot all be right, but they might all be wrong; or, taken on their own, partially true but inadequate. Historical investigation

---

36 For an example of a similar list see John Dominic Crossan, *The Historical Jesus*, HarperCollins 1992.

has not brought unanimity but rather confusion and controversy. Compared to the rich, dynamic and multi-faceted picture of Jesus in the canonical Gospels, these historical reconstructions appear one-dimensional and ultimately, for me, both unsatisfying and unconvincing. So Douglas, where does this leave us?

In the Old Testament story there is often a sense of urgency. God is portrayed as one who seeks, pursues, confronts, challenges, exhorts, calls and comforts his people. The first question God asks in Scripture is addressed to Adam – 'Where are you?' (Genesis 3:9). As Adam stands for 'everyman,' here the question is also addressed to us. In the Gospels, the challenge of Jesus, 'Come follow me' (Matthew 4:19) is also given within a framework of urgency. This is depicted as a monumental decision that cannot be put off. To ignore or reject this summons is to be in danger of missing the boat; of being left behind.

Perhaps it is only truly in times of crisis we can sense the power of this urgency which lies behind the Biblical texts. The great German Protestant Theologian and Pastor Helmut Thielicke lived through the horrors of WW2. He stood in opposition to the Nazis and was arrested by the Gestapo on five separate occasions. During the Allied bombing of Stuttgart, he preached each week on the Lord's Prayer. One morning, inspecting the damage in the city, he stood at the edge of a crater looking down into the hole that had been a shelter for fifty people the night before. A woman came to his side and obviously recognised him. She said, 'My husband died down there. Unfortunately there was no trace left of him only his cap.' Thielicke was about to express his sorrow when she continued, 'We heard your last sermon in the Church. I want to thank you for preparing my husband for eternity.' Questions of faith certainly take on a different magnitude of importance whilst standing at the 'crater's edge.'[37]

Your friend Jordan Peterson's response to questions regarding his own faith – 'living as if it were true' – is perhaps the only

---

37 Helmut Thielicke, *The Prayer That Spans The World* , James Clarke and Co. Ltd 1978, pp. 65, 66.

realistic starting point for us all. Of course, such a step of faith is only possible for those who already have some empathy with and openness towards the Christian story in the first place. In a very real and practical sense, the Christian story is a 'proclamation.' When that proclamation evokes 'resonance' within the hearer, then Christian pilgrimage can begin. I sense that the story is still alive to you in subtle and profound ways. Perhaps Douglas, like the French philosopher Paul Ricoeur, you need a 'second naïveté' to awaken a childlike (but certainly not childish) wonder and trust in the Gospel of the Nazarene.[38] But then, don't we all!

Thank you Douglas, for who you are and what you do.
May God bless you on the journey.

---

38 Cf. the words of Jesus in Matthew 18: 3.

The Handsel Press is a not-for-profit company owned by the Handsel Trust. See: https://handselpress.co.uk/

To purchase books, go to: https://buy.sanctusmedia.com/ store/collections/handsel-press-store (or google 'Sanctus Media Handsel Press').

The editor can be contacted at: jstein@handselpress.org.uk.